A Blue Collar Answer to Protestantism

John Martignoni

A Blue Collar Answer to Protestantism

Catholic Questions Protestants Can't Answer

Foreword by Johnnette Benkovic Williams

EWTN PUBLISHING, INC.
Irondale, Alabama

Unless otherwise noted, biblical references in this book are taken from the *Revised Standard Version Bible: Catholic Edition*, copyright © 1989, 1993 National Council of the Churches of Christ in the United States of America. Used by permission. All rights reserved worldwide.

EWTN Publishing, Inc.
5817 Old Leeds Road, Irondale, AL 35210

Distributed by Sophia Institute Press, Box 5284, Manchester, NH 03108.

paperback ISBN 978-1-68278-295-8
ebook ISBN 978-1-68278-296-5
Library of Congress Control Number: 2023942782

First printing

Acknowledgments

I wish to thank all those—too numerous to mention individually—from whom I have learned anything at all about the Catholic Faith, whether they be living or dead, in this century or in any of the previous 20 centuries. I wish to thank God, Who has given me all that I have, but, in particular, for the two gifts He has given me that have proven quite useful for this work in apologetics—a thick skin and a thick skull. And I wish to thank my parents—Pasquale and Florence Martignoni—for giving me life and a stable and loving home to grow up in and in which to thrive.

Contents

PART 2
Questions Protestants Can't Answer

Contents

Foreword

We live in a day and time when logic and "good 'ol common sense" are at a premium. Ask someone why he believes what he does, and he is often ill-equipped to back it up with sound reasoning. Question him a bit more and the reply is likely to be, "Well, that's just how I feel." And while it is necessary to acknowledge our emotions, it is the intellect that ought to govern our decisions and practices, especially those that relate to our relationship with God and our eternal destiny.

This is why John Martignoni's work is so important. He focuses his attention on providing a cogent, reasoned, sound argument for the truths of the Faith and aids others in doing the same. John is an accomplished apologist, student of Scripture, and founder of an apostolate dedicated to a scriptural defense of the Faith. We saw his skill and precision in his first book, *Blue Collar Apologetics*, and I've had the good pleasure of interviewing him on it several times via television and radio. It is one of the most useful and engaging apologetics books I have read.

In this his latest work, *A Blue Collar Answer to Protestantism*, John begins to uncover the incoherence of Protestant doctrine by looking at its key teachings, most significantly *Sola Scriptura* and *Sola Fide*. Using Sacred Scripture as his lens, he cites one passage after another that refutes the notion that Scripture is the sole teacher of truth and that only faith is required for salvation. He delves into other doctrinal problems with Protestantism as well. By revealing the inconsistency and lack of logical development in the distinctly Protestant theological concepts, his readers come to a deeper appreciation of the inherent continuity and development of Church teaching from its founding by Jesus Christ to the present day. And they also come to see how the seed of truth of every Catholic teaching is rooted in Sacred Scripture.

In the second half of his book, John offers a compendium of questions that stump Protestants. These come from his own experience as a defender of the Faith in debates with Protestants. I found these to be engrossing and educational. The goal, of course, is not to embarrass nor to insult, but rather to lead and to guide. I'm confident they will be helpful to me in responding to questions I am asked personally as well as in giving advice and counsel to radio callers and listeners. This book, along with *Blue Collar Apologetics*, are two references I will use often.

As we see the condition of our current culture, as we watch family members and friends wandering off to fables and to other religious expressions, it is good we have tools to help us remain firm in our faith and to aid us in leading others to the fullness of Truth that is ours in our Catholic Faith. *A Blue Collar Answer to Protestantism* does both. Gratitude to you, John, for your help and assistance!

Johnnette Benkovic Williams
Founder and President of *Women of Grace*®
EWTN Television and Radio Host

A Blue Collar Answer to Protestantism

Introduction

The exclusive focus of this book, as you can probably tell from the title, is Protestantism — specifically the errors found within Protestantism. Errors in doctrine and dogma, to be sure, but also errors in just plain old logic. Protestantism, as a theological system, is scripturally and logically inconsistent, which renders it, essentially, incoherent.

And when I say that Protestantism is incoherent, I want to make it clear that I am not saying there is absolutely nothing within Protestantism that makes sense. What I am saying, rather, is that those doctrines and dogmas of Protestantism that are distinctly Protestant — such as *Sola Scriptura*, *Sola Fide*, "Once Saved, Always Saved," the Rapture, and so on (the ones that they have *not* borrowed from Catholicism) — simply do not make sense from the perspective of Scripture or the perspective of logic.

The incoherence of Protestant doctrine and dogma — the lack of "sense" in them — is exactly what I will demonstrate in this book. While there are many apologetics books out there that make the arguments for this or that Catholic teaching and against this or that Protestant teaching — my previous book, *Blue Collar Apologetics*, is an example — this book comes at Protestant teaching from a slightly different angle.

In the first half of this book, I am going to explore some problems with Protestantism by looking more at the forest instead of the trees. What I mean by that is there are inconsistencies inherent in

Protestantism that one doesn't necessarily see when arguing against this or that individual doctrine. But when you look at the whole of Protestantism and Protestant theology, and apply a little logic and some common sense, those inconsistencies become rather apparent.

So, instead of using Scripture and the writings of the Church Fathers and so on to just argue against all of the various Protestant doctrines individually, I'm going to apply a little logic and some common sense to show, in a broader sense, that Protestantism as a whole, and in its foundational pillars—*Sola Scriptura* and *Sola Fide*—makes no sense. It makes no common sense, it makes no logical sense, and most importantly, it makes no biblical sense, even though most Protestants claim that they go by the Bible, and the Bible alone. Using logic and common sense to examine, from a macro perspective, some of the unspoken and unexamined premises that underpin all of Protestant theology, you can again see some inconsistencies that are not necessarily obvious when you just deal with all of the individual doctrines and dogmas one at a time.

In the second half of this book, I am going to look more at the individual trees instead of the forest. I'm going to zero in on specific teachings within Protestant theology. I'll do this by asking pointed questions that are, for the most part, based on a Scripture verse, and which Protestants have probably never heard before and, therefore, have never even considered.

Socrates once said that the unexamined life isn't worth living. I would borrow that sentiment and apply it to theology by saying that the unexamined doctrine isn't worth believing. These questions I ask are designed to make the Protestant believer think about what it is they believe and why they believe it. And as the title of the book states, I contend that these are questions Protestants can't answer. Oh, they can give some sort of answer, but their answers will not be logically or scripturally consistent with their system of theology. Their answers will either contradict Scripture or contradict their theology, one or the other. I guarantee it.

These questions will revolve around just a few of the most central Protestant doctrines—particularly *Sola Scriptura* and *Sola Fide*, which, as I alluded to above, I call the two "pillars of Protestantism"—and will also touch on a Catholic doctrine here and there. So you will, for example, have several questions on *Sola Fide*, but each question will give a slightly different nuance of argument against *Sola Fide* arising from Scripture itself or simple logic. I've done this because I believe it is important to show that the arguments against Protestant doctrines are deep and wide and valid from any number of different perspectives provided by Scripture, simple logic, and from the perspective of that exceedingly rare trait these days—common sense.

Also, while I could come up with similar questions, in large numbers, for pretty much every Protestant doctrine, there really is no need to. If I can demonstrate that the main dogmas of Protestantism—in particular, the two pillars of Protestantism—are not worthy of belief, then that entire system of theology comes crumbling down.

Now, there are probably those of you who would object: "John, why do you focus so much on Protestants? After all, they're Christians. Why not try to evangelize Mormons, Jews, Muslims, Buddhists, Hindus, or atheists? Don't they need to hear about Jesus more than the Protestants do?" I would offer three points in response for you to consider:

1. Evangelizing non-Catholic Christians does not mean one cannot also evangelize non-Christians. The two propositions are not mutually exclusive.

2. Jesus says that a house divided against itself cannot stand (Mark 3:25). Right now, the Christian "house" is divided against itself, and it is, as a result, suffering horrendous casualties. There are tens of thousands upon tens of thousands of divisions within Christianity. These divisions make our witness much less effective to those in non-Christian religions and to those with no religion, not to mention those within our own house. And these divisions tend to render ineffective our witness to the culture as a whole, which is why we have so many of the societal ills that we are plagued with today, because the Church does not speak with one, clear, bold,

and unequivocal voice. We need to have one church with one message — not tens of thousands of churches with tens of thousands of messages — if we are to survive and stand as an authentic witness to the world.

3. Truth matters. Jesus tells us that He is the Truth (John 14:6), that He came into the world to bear witness to the truth and that everyone who is of the truth hears His voice (John 18:37), and that the truth will make us free (John 8:32). Paul tells us that God wants all men to come to the knowledge of the truth (1 Tim. 2:4). The Catholic Church has the fullness of the truth as given to us by Jesus Christ. The Church is the fullness of Him who fills all in all (Eph. 1:23). Which means all other Christian faith traditions have, at best, partial truth. Well, I want them to have the fullness of the truth. I want them to have the fullness of Jesus Christ. I want them to have what we have. I want them to receive Jesus Christ, Body, Blood, Soul, and Divinity, in the Eucharist.

That is why I focus so much on Protestants: so that by us Christians becoming truly one, as Jesus prayed we should be, the world may then believe that Jesus was sent by God for the salvation of all (John 17:21).

I want to make it clear that I use the term *Protestant* to denote all those faith traditions that use the sixty-six-book Protestant Bible. They do not belong to either the Catholic Church or to one of the Orthodox Churches. Whether they be Lutheran, Anglican, Methodist, Presbyterian, Baptist, evangelical, Pentecostal, Church of Christ, nondenominational, or so on, I refer to all of them as Protestant. This is done, first and foremost, simply for ease of discussion. Some in these groups might object to being referred to as Protestants, but again, I am doing so simply to avoid having to repeat a long list of denominational names every time I am speaking about non-Catholic, non-Orthodox Christian faith traditions. Plus, the reality is that all of these groups, whether they realize it or not, trace their spiritual heritage back to one or more of the founders of Protestantism — Martin Luther, Calvin,

Zwingli, Henry VIII, and others. And again, they have in common that they all use the sixty-six-book Protestant Bible. If the Protestant Bible is your Bible, you are, essentially, Protestant.

As you read through this book, you will realize that there is some redundancy in it. You will encounter certain themes more than once, and maybe several times. This is done with a purpose in mind. As I mentioned above, I want to show that the arguments against Protestant theology, as a whole and in its parts, can be brought from many different angles, perspectives, and Scripture verses. So you will see questions about *Sola Fide* for example, being asked in several different ways and rising up from many different verses from Scripture. I want to demonstrate that the arguments against Protestantism flow out of not just a few Scripture verses here or there but all parts of Scripture.

Finally, as I said in the introduction to my previous book, if you are looking to find deep theology or deep philosophy in these pages, please stop reading right now. Some folks who consider themselves "theologians" or "philosophers" will undoubtedly think this book to be overly simplistic. Essentially, I would have to agree with them.

The problems and questions that I bring up in the following pages are based on, again, what I consider to be basic common sense and simple logic. As I've talked to, or corresponded with, literally a few thousand Protestants over the last twenty-five years or so, there have been a number of times where, in the middle of the conversation, I've thought to myself, "Wait a minute, that can't be right. That doesn't make any sense." So, in order to try and point out the problems and contradictions in what I was hearing, I asked questions of the folks with whom I was dialoguing—the questions in this book (and many that aren't in this book). And most of these questions have never received a straightforward, rational, logical answer that is consistent with both Scripture and Protestant theology, even though I have asked them many times. Thus, the title of the book. I hope you enjoy it.

PART 1

Problems with Protestantism

1

Decapitating Jesus

In Protestantism, there is a tendency to separate Jesus from the Church. I have heard time and time again from any number of Protestants that they don't need a church as long as they have Jesus and their Bible. I have also been told, many times, I should go by what the Bible says and not by what the Church says. "Listen to the Bible, not the Church." They say the Church is simply a place to go to fellowship and worship with other Christians and that it is not necessary for their salvation. For them, Jesus is necessary, but the Church is not. For them, the Bible is necessary (it tells all about Jesus and the salvation He offers), but the Church is not. I refer to this tendency of separating Jesus from the Church—pitting the Bible against the Church—as "decapitating Jesus."

Decapitating Jesus. That's a fairly stark phrase, but intentionally so. I hope to jar people's sensibilities just a bit to get them thinking about what it is they believe and why they believe it. So, why do I say that Protestantism decapitates Jesus? Let me start the explanation with a passage from Scripture: "And from his fulness have we all received, grace upon grace" (John 1:16). Again, what does that passage tell us? It tells us we have received, from the fullness of Jesus Christ, grace upon grace. Grace comes to us from the fullness of Jesus Christ. I think everyone—Catholic and Protestant—would agree with that. I mean, that's what the Bible very clearly states.

Okay, then, let's look at another Bible passage: "For in him [Jesus] all the fulness of God was pleased to dwell" (Col. 1:19). And in Colossians

2:9–10, it says this: "For in him [Jesus] the whole fulness of deity dwells bodily, and you have come to fulness of life in him, who is the head of all rule and authority." Fullness is the theme here. The fullness of deity dwells bodily in Jesus Christ. And we have received, as it says in John 1:16, grace after grace from this fullness. Again, I believe both Catholics and Protestants would agree with that 100 percent.

But this actually presents a bit of a problem for those Protestants who pit Jesus and the Bible against the Church. How so, you might ask? Well, because of what it says in Ephesians 1:22–23: "And he [the Father] has put all things under his [Jesus'] feet and has made him the head over all things for the church, which is his body, the fulness of him who fills all in all."

Did you catch that? The Church, according to the Word of God, is the "fulness" of Jesus Christ. From where does the Bible—the Word of God—say that we get grace upon grace? From the "fulness" of Jesus Christ (John 1:16). And what is the "fulness" of Jesus Christ, according to the Word of God? The Church! And from where does the Bible—the Word of God—say we get the fullness of life? From the "fulness" of deity in Him (Jesus). And what is the "fulness" of Jesus Christ, according to the Word of God? The Church! So if grace upon grace and fullness of life come from the fullness of Jesus Christ, and the Church is the fullness of Jesus Christ, then where do we get grace upon grace and the fullness of life? The Church, which is the Body of Christ, the "fulness" of Him who fills all in all.

If the Church is the Body of Christ, Who is the Head of the Body? Jesus Christ (see Eph. 1:22–23). And how does the Word of God describe what Jesus is the Head over? The Word of God says He is the Head of "all rule and authority" (Col. 2:9–10). So, Jesus is the Head over the Body, which is the Church, which is "all rule and authority." So, where do we find rule and authority? In the Church, which is the Body of Christ.

The argument of finding the authority of Jesus Christ Himself in the Church is further strengthened by Scripture when you look at Matthew 18:15–18, where Jesus tells the apostles to take disputes to the binding authority of the Church for a decision. The Church that has the authority, from Jesus Christ Himself, to bind and loose on earth that which then shall be bound and loosed in Heaven. In other words, the Church has to be infallible in Her judgment because whatever it is binding and loosing on earth is being bound and loosed in Heaven by God. God does not bind and loose error. Therefore, the Church's judgments in these matters have to be free from error—that is, infallible.

So, where does all of this get us? For Protestants, the answer is that it gets you in a lot of theological trouble. I once dialogued with an evangelical pastor in my e-newsletter, *Apologetics for the Masses*, who said that all authority that he has—to preach, to teach, to pastor, and so on—comes directly to him from Jesus Christ through the Scriptures, *not* through the Church. First of all, nowhere does the Bible ever say such a thing. Second, the Scriptures tell us that all authority of Jesus Christ, grace upon grace through Jesus Christ, and fullness of life in Jesus Christ come through the fullness of Jesus Christ. The fullness of Jesus Christ that is identified as *the Church*.

The thing is, though, I don't believe that pastor, or any Protestant minister or layperson, would ever claim that his church is the fullness of Jesus Christ and that one receives grace upon grace through his church and that all rule and authority of Jesus Christ resides in his church. This particular pastor had already said all authority resides in the Bible, and he isn't alone in his belief. Yet the Bible says all authority resides in the Body of Christ—the Church. So, who do you believe, the Word of God or the Word of Pastor X?

That is why, when so many Protestants pit the Bible against the Church, pit Jesus against the Church, what they are actually doing is removing the Head (Jesus) from the Body (the Church). They are, in essence, decapitating Jesus. When Protestants adopt a "me-and-Jesus" theology, when they say that you don't need the Church as long as you've got the Bible, when they say that the Church isn't necessary for one's salvation, they are essentially cutting Jesus' Head off from His Body. They are saying that you don't need the Body of Christ for salvation, you just need His Head.

The Church is the Mystical Body of Christ. Jesus identifies with His Church as one and the same. We see this in Ephesians 5:31–32, where Paul uses the language of marriage to say that Jesus and the Church are one. We see it in Acts 9:4, where Jesus asks Saul, "Why do you persecute me?" Who was Paul persecuting? Acts 8:3 says, "Saul laid waste the church." Saul was persecuting the Church. Jesus asks him, "Why do you persecute me?" Jesus and the Church are one.

All those Protestants who downplay the role of the Church, and even sometimes look at the Church with disdain, are in grave danger of losing their salvation. Why? Because you cannot have Jesus if you don't have the Church. You cannot have the Head if you do not have the Body. The Bible makes that very plain. Jesus and the Church are one. Separating the Church from Jesus, pitting the Bible against the Church, is cutting the Head off the Body. It is a catastrophic mistake.

Now, one argument that a Protestant might come back with is this: "Well, yes, we agree that Jesus and the Church are one, but the Church here is not the Catholic Church!" Fine, for the sake of argument, let's say it's not the Catholic Church. But that still doesn't fix the Protestants' problem. Because if it's not the Catholic Church, then that means there is some church out there that is the "fulness" of Jesus Christ and has been the fullness of Christ since it was founded 2,000 years ago. There is some church out there from which one has been able to receive grace upon grace for 2,000 years. There is some church out there from which one could receive fullness of life for 2,000 years. There is some church out there that has wielded the authority of Jesus Christ Himself for 2,000 years. There is some church out there that has been binding and loosing on earth that which is bound and loosed in Heaven for 2,000 years. There is some church out there that has had the gift of infallibility as it operated with the authority of Jesus Christ for 2,000 years.

So, if it's not the Catholic Church, which church is it? Well, it's definitely not the church of the pastor I spoke of earlier. After all, that pastor denies that any earthly authority could be infallible. Plus, he says authority, grace, and life are bestowed upon him by the Bible, not by the Church. And he has admitted that his church is only 150 years old. The Church that is the Body of Christ has to be—*has to be!*—2,000 years old. So, which church is it?

Well, we have to eliminate as a possibility all the Protestant churches that deny they wield the infallible authority of Jesus Christ. We have to eliminate as a possibility all of the Protestant churches that have never claimed to bind and loose things on earth that are also bound and loosed in Heaven. We have to eliminate as a possibility all Protestant churches that are not 2,000 years old. We have to eliminate all Protestant churches that claim you receive grace and fullness of life and authority through the Bible and not the Church. In other words, we have to eliminate as a possibility all Protestant churches—period—since not a single Protestant church matches any of these criteria!

To sum up, the Protestant "me-and-Jesus" theology that relegates the Church to this amorphous concept of all those who have accepted Jesus Christ as their "personal Lord and Savior," regardless of what church they belong to, is a lifeless theology that could very well lead one to destruction. It is a theology that makes the Church essentially irrelevant to salvation—in opposition to the theology that embraces the Church described in Scripture as the fullness of Jesus Christ, which has all authority and through which grace upon grace and fullness of life is received. It is a theology that decapitates Jesus. It is a fatal flaw in Protestantism.

It is a problem with Protestantism.

2

What's Love Got to Do With It?

In Protestant theology, one of the two main dogmas is *Sola Fide*—salvation by faith alone. And I want to emphasize the word *alone*. That is the belief that all I have to do is believe that Jesus is God incarnate and that He died on the Cross for my sins and (BOOM!) I'm saved. I don't have to do any works. I don't have to be baptized. I don't have to worry about sacraments or growing in holiness or anything else. All I have to do—the *only* thing I have to do—the only thing I can do or that anyone can do that counts for anything is to have faith. I am saved by my faith, and by my faith alone. Period!

The dogma of *Sola Fide* invites the question asked by Tina Turner: What's love got to do with it? What role does love play in my salvation? Well, that's a pretty easy question to answer. If we are saved by faith, and faith alone, then by definition, love has absolutely nothing to do with our salvation. I mean, c'mon, it's right there in the name of the dogma—SOLA Fide—Faith ALONE. That's a pretty easy thing to figure out.

But given what the Word of God says about love, can that really be right? Does that make scriptural sense? I mean, Jesus—the King of kings and Lord of lords—tells us that the two greatest commandments are to love God with all our heart, soul, and mind and to love your neighbor as yourself (Matt. 22:37–39). The Word of God tells us that God is Love (1 John 4:8, 16). "Faith, hope, and love abide, these three; but the greatest of these is love" (1 Cor. 13:13). "For in Christ Jesus neither circumcision nor uncircumcision is of any avail, but faith working through love" (Gal. 5:6).

Love, love, love. And more love. Yet love, according to Protestant *Sola Fide* theology, has nothing to do with our salvation. It is faith *alone* that saves us, which means that I don't have to love my neighbor as myself, and I'm still saved as long as I've accepted Jesus into my heart as my personal Lord and Savior. After all, loving my neighbor falls into the category of works, and works don't save us, right? Shoot, I don't even have to love God, and I'm still saved as long as I've accepted Jesus into my heart as my personal Lord and Savior. So, I don't have to keep the two greatest commandments—or any commandment for that matter (after all, keeping a commandment is a work)—and I'm still saved as long as I've accepted Jesus into my heart as my personal Lord and Savior. How awesome is that!

Sola Fide theology turns so many passages of Scripture on their head that I have trouble understanding why anyone who actually reads the Bible could believe in it. Feeding the hungry, clothing the naked, visiting the sick and imprisoned (i.e., loving my neighbor as myself; Matt. 25:45–46)—I don't have to do any of those things, and I'm still saved regardless of what the Bible says. And how can love be greater than faith when salvation is the greatest thing we can achieve and having faith, not love, is the only way to achieve it? Faith has to be greater than love if *Sola Fide* is true. "If you love me, you will keep my commandments" (John 14:15). Well, I obviously don't need to keep the commandments because I don't need to love Jesus in order to be saved.

"For God so loved the world that he gave his only Son, that whoever believes in him should not perish but have eternal life" (John 3:16). Awesome! God loves me. He loves me so much that I don't have to do a thing—not one dadgum thing—other than believe in Him to be saved. He loves me, but I don't have to love Him, and I'm still saved. I can sin all I want, and as long as I have accepted Jesus into my heart as my personal Lord and Savior, I'm saved. And who was it that said the road to salvation is narrow and difficult? Silly rabbit, no it's not; it's pretty easy actually.

Now, someone might say, as they have said to me in the past, "John, you're being ridiculous. That's not what *Sola Fide* folks believe." My first point in response is this: It is indeed what a number of them actually believe. They may not frame it in the exact manner that I have, but based on their actions and their words, it is indeed what they believe. That's why adultery is not a salvation issue. Cheating and lying and stealing are not salvation issues. Watching pornography is not a salvation issue. Engaging in extramarital sex is not a salvation issue. Having an abortion is not a salvation issue. Breaking the commandments is not a salvation issue. Not loving your neighbor is not a salvation issue. Ignoring the poor, the hungry, the sick, and the imprisoned is not a salvation issue. And I could go on and on and on. Name a sin—other than unbelief—and ask a Protestant who believes in *Sola Fide* if committing that sin is a salvation issue. They will tell you it's not as long as you believe.

My second point in response to the argument that I'm just being ridiculous is it doesn't matter if they believe these things I'm saying or not. The things I have said above are the logical consequence of the dogma of *Sola Fide*, whether *Sola Fide* adherents personally go that far with it or not (I just think a lot of them have never actually taken the time to think through the logical consequences of this dogma). I have had a *Sola Fide* believer look me straight in the eye and tell me, "No, you don't have to love God in order to be saved." That's because he was honest enough to admit that being saved by faith, and faith alone, rules out the possibility of love having anything to do with your salvation. Again, if faith alone saves you, then that means, by definition, that love has nothing—zero, zip, nada, *nothing*—to do with your salvation. That is the logic that is built into the dogma itself. Because if love does have something to do with our salvation, then we are not saved by faith alone, and the dogma of *Sola Fide* falls apart. And if the dogma falls apart, then everyone who believes in *Sola Fide* would have to take a good long look at the Catholic Church because we have always taught that love is necessary for salvation.

Think about it: salvation by faith alone precludes love from having anything to do with our salvation. Yes, God has to love us, but we don't have to love Him or any of His creation to still be eligible for salvation.

One argument people have made in response to what I've said here is this: "Well, if you don't love the Lord or do the works of the Lord, then that means you haven't really accepted Him into your heart as your personal Lord and Savior, and you weren't really saved in the first place." My response: Really? Where does the Bible tell me such a thing? Where does the Bible say, "If you don't do the works of the Lord, then that means you were never really saved in the first place"? Someone might answer me by pointing to James 2:14–18, but those verses are saying that faith without works—that is, faith alone (*Sola Fide*)—is dead; it cannot save you. They are not saying that if you don't demonstrate your love for God and others by not doing good works, then it proves you never had faith to begin with.

Furthermore, how many works do I have to do to prove that I have truly accepted Jesus into my heart as my personal Lord and Savior? Ten? Twenty? Five years' worth? Ten years' worth? How many works does it take to prove that you're saved?

Sorry, but that is a specious argument. The Bible doesn't say it, and if the Bible doesn't say it, I don't have to believe it (*Sola Scriptura*), right? Again, if faith *alone* saves us, then inherent in the dogma is the fact that love doesn't have anything to do with it.

Another argument I've heard to counter what I've been saying here is that, yes, a person who doesn't love God or his neighbor can be saved by accepting Jesus into his heart as his personal Lord and Savior. But if he is *truly* saved, if he *really* accepted Jesus into his heart, then he will just naturally grow to love God and his fellow man, and he will do the good works the Bible speaks of out of love for God and man.

My first response to that argument is: You do realize that you just agreed with me that love has nothing to do with one's salvation under a *Sola Fide* theological system, right? My second response is: Where does the Bible say that if you are *truly* saved, you will, sort of automatically, grow in love of God and your fellow man? When speaking to the Church (the believers) of Ephesus, Jesus says they have "abandoned" the love and the works that they did at first (Rev. 2:1–5). How is that possible if, after you're saved, you just naturally grow in love for God and your fellow man? Does that mean that they weren't really saved in the first place? Did they need to reaccept Jesus into their hearts as their personal Lord and Savior to get *truly* saved?

You just can't argue that love plays a role in one's salvation when you believe that salvation is by faith alone. Again, inherent in the definition of the dogma of *Sola Fide* is the fact that love plays no role whatsoever in a person's salvation. If you believe that love somehow does play a role in a person's salvation, then it is not salvation by faith alone. It is salvation by faith and love or, as Galatians 5:6 says, "faith working through love."

What's love got to do with it is a problem with Protestantism.

3

Binding and Loosing

Jesus said to Peter, "I will give you the keys of the kingdom of heaven, and whatever you bind on earth shall be bound in heaven, and whatever you loose on earth shall be loosed in heaven" (Matt. 16:19). Here we see the power of binding and loosing in the context of the keys of the Kingdom of Heaven being bestowed upon Peter.

In Matthew 18:18, Jesus bestows the power of binding and loosing upon not just Peter but other disciples — other leaders of the Church — as well. This time, it is done in the context of the Church being the ultimate arbiter of disputes between Christians: "Tell it to the church; and if he refuses to listen even to the church, let him be to you as a Gentile and a tax collector" (Matt. 18:17).

In both Matthew 16 and 18, the power of binding and loosing has to do with authority. As the *Catechism of the Catholic Church* states, binding and loosing refers, primarily, to three different things: "The power to 'bind and loose' connotes the authority to absolve sins, to pronounce doctrinal judgments, and to make disciplinary decisions in the Church" (no. 553).

The fact that binding and loosing is a function of authority is a problem with Protestantism because, in all of Protestantism, there is no one who has the authority to bind and loose on earth what is then bound and loosed in Heaven in all three of these areas just mentioned. Yes, Protestant leaders can make disciplinary decisions in their churches and denominations, but the vast majority of them will not even claim the authority to absolve sins (exceptions can be found in the Lutheran and Anglican denominations). And I don't know of a single Protestant denomination that claims there is anyone in that denomination who can pronounce on doctrinal matters in a way that is authoritatively binding on all other members of Protestantism, or even, for that matter, that is authoritatively binding upon the members of their own particular denomination. That is why when you read about binding and loosing as taught by Protestants, it is generally referring to those terms in a context related to disciplinary decisions and not to doctrinal issues or the forgiveness of sin.

There are some Protestants, though, who will say that they can indeed bind and loose in regard to sins, but they are referring to either the sins that a person has committed against them personally, to which they can say, "I forgive you" or "I don't forgive you," or kicking someone out of their congregation for obstinacy in sin or allowing someone back into their congregation after that person has been forced out or shunned or excommunicated. But in essence, this latter rendering of binding and loosing is all about enforcing or remanding a disciplinary action against a member of the congregation. It is not truly about the forgiveness of sin. And the former rendering of binding and loosing is simply referring to my forgiving you for sinning against me, but it has nothing to do with the actual forgiveness or absolution of your sin in the eyes of God.

Again, neither of the perspectives on binding and loosing regarding sin refer to the absolving of sins in the eyes of God such as what Jesus did with the paralytic in Matthew 9:1–9. "Take heart, my son; your sins are forgiven" (v. 2). And this authority—the "authority on earth to forgive sins" (v. 6), to absolve sins as God absolves sins—is said to be given not just to one man, Jesus Christ, but to "men" plural (v. 8). The Bible is telling us that "men" have the authority on earth to forgive sins in the same manner that Jesus forgave sins in Matthew 9. This is what Jesus was doing in John 20:21–23 when He said to the apostles, "If you forgive the sins of any, they are forgiven [loosed]; if you retain the sins of any, they are retained [bound]." He was giving them the authority on earth to forgive or retain sins. He was giving them the authority of binding and loosing regarding the forgiveness of sin.

And in both Matthew 9 and John 20, the Bible isn't talking about just me forgiving you if you've wronged me somehow. No, it's talking about men having the authority to forgive the sins of others who have committed sins against God. It's talking about the authority to forgive sins as God forgives sins. That is what the binding and loosing regarding the forgiveness of sins is all about. If I have that authority to bind and loose, then it means if I forgive you of your sins (loose), then God has also forgiven you of your sins. And just as importantly, if I do not forgive you of your sins (bind), then neither has God forgiven you of your sins. Protestantism, with a few exceptions, generally claims no such authority.

Protestants will also say that they do indeed have the authority to pronounce doctrinal judgments. Yes, but not doctrinal judgments that are actually binding on all Protestants. No authority in Protestantism would even make the claim to be able to do so. Do you know why? Because no authority in Protestantism will make the claim of infallibility. (Although, as I have said many times, they may not claim to be infallible, they will most definitely act as if they are infallible, especially when it comes to their discussions with Catholics.) And if you are not infallible when making a doctrinal claim, then your doctrinal claim is only as good as your ability to convince other people that they should listen to you.

That's a problem with Protestantism. Because the authority of binding and loosing has the authority of Heaven itself behind it but no Protestant can claim such authority behind their personal fallible decisions, no Protestant actually has the authority of binding and loosing regarding matters of doctrine. Again, this is a problem because God gave His Church the authority to bind and loose, and He put His infallible authority behind this binding and loosing. This is why many Protestants argue that the authority to bind and loose died out with the apostles. They inherently recognize that there is no such authority in Protestantism, so they just say it no longer exists. How convenient. (Note: the Bible nowhere says the Church's power of binding and loosing ends with the death of the last apostle.) So, if the leaders of your church cannot claim the authority of God Himself and all of Heaven behind their doctrinal binding and loosing—God saying whatever they bind on earth He will bind in Heaven and whatever they loose on earth He will loose in Heaven—then you need to realize that you are not in the Church founded by Jesus Christ.

If a statement of doctrine is bound or loosed by God Himself, that statement of doctrine is necessarily infallible in its essence. God would not bind or loose an error—any error. We see this in Acts 15 with the Council of Jerusalem. The statement of the council was infallible in its essence because, as it says in Acts 15:28, the decision of the council was not just the decision of the Church leaders gathered there but also the decision of the Holy Spirit that was effected through the decision of Peter and the other leaders of the Church.

Do you know of any Protestant council, assembly, bishop, pastor, theologian, or board of deacons that claims to be infallible in its pronouncements? Is there any Protestant council, assembly, bishop, pastor, theologian, or board of deacons that can say, "It seemed good to the Holy Spirit and to us," when they make a doctrinal decision? There is none. Therefore, there can be no binding and loosing authority regarding doctrinal pronouncements. This, again, is why the topic is generally avoided in Protestant discussions of binding and loosing.

Some Protestants will try to get around all of this by saying, "Well, the translations used in most Bibles in Matthew 16:19 and 18:18 are bad translations." They claim that those verses should read something along the lines of: "Whatever has already been bound in Heaven, you will bind on earth, and whatever has already been loosed in Heaven, you will loose on earth." In other words, they claim God is not binding and loosing after the fact what has been bound and loosed on earth; rather, His ministers on earth are binding and loosing what God has already bound or loosed in Heaven. If we only knew the Greek better, we would all realize that. So, binding and loosing, they claim, has nothing to do with infallibility. It has nothing to do with some supposed authority of a person here on earth that God then puts His stamp on.

For the sake of argument, let's concede the point. Let's say that those verses are not correctly translated or correctly understood. That does not, however, overcome the problem with Protestantism. If you claim you are binding and loosing something on earth that God has already bound or loosed in Heaven, then you are still claiming that whatever proclamation you are making is infallible because it has the authority of God and Heaven behind it. You are also claiming that God has somehow conveyed this decision of His to bind or loose something in Heaven to you in an infallible manner. Did He appear to you? Send an angel? Email? Call? Text? Perhaps He sent Mary to you. Well, never mind on that one. How did God inform you? So, if you bind the people in your congregation on earth to believe this or that doctrine or to go to church on Wednesday night as well as on Sunday morning, are you saying that God has given you "a word," infallibly telling you that He has already bound this in Heaven? That's basically the position they are left with.

Some may claim that it was through the Bible that God told them what He has already bound and loosed in Heaven. Sorry, but that still doesn't solve the Protestants' problem. That means that you have infallibly interpreted the Bible, which means you are infallible in your doctrinal pronouncements. But again, Protestants don't claim infallibility. So, we're back to square one.

Do you, Mr. Protestant, claim that all of the authority and power of God is behind your pronouncements on doctrine? No? Then you do not have the power of binding and loosing.

Do you, Mr. Protestant, claim that all of the authority and power of God is behind your forgiving or retaining the sins of others? No? Then you do not have the power of binding and loosing.

If you claim that neither of those is related to the authority of binding and loosing, then I will ask: Do you, Mr. Protestant, claim that all of the authority and power of God is behind your pronouncements on disciplinary decisions? Yes? Then please tell me how you know this is so whenever you bind or loose regarding some matter of discipline within your congregation. And would you say your disciplinary action is infallible? Of course you won't!

All of this is why the Lord giving His Church the authority to bind and loose results in a problem with Protestantism. Can you name one thing that a particular Protestant leader, or group of leaders, has claimed to infallibly bind upon all Christians? I mean, if the authority of Heaven is behind their binding and loosing, wouldn't it apply to all Christians?

So, in Protestantism, there is no binding and loosing that can be pointed to as applying to all Christians, or even just to all Protestants. There is no one who can bind and loose regarding doctrine. There is no one who can bind and loose regarding the forgiveness of sins in the eyes of God. There is no claim of infallibility that would enable one to claim the force of Heaven behind any supposed binding and loosing. In other words, there is no binding and loosing in Protestantism; yet Jesus gave His Church the authority to bind and loose.

One last thought on this matter, and this is an important point to make, is the fact that no individual Protestant that I have ever talked to—and that number is in the thousands—recognizes his or her leaders as having the authority to bind and loose on anything other than a disciplinary matter or maybe to add a kitchen to the church building or elect a new deacon or put in a new dress code or some such action. Although, even in disciplinary matters, few, if any, Protestants would recognize their leaders as having binding and loosing authority that is backed by Heaven. I have heard, for example, of Protestant congregations that have split over things as minor as whether or not the men should wear coats and ties to the Sunday worship service. Obviously, those folks didn't feel their pastor had the power to bind and loose, even in a disciplinary matter.

But the main point I want to make here is that Protestant ministers definitely do not have the authority to bind and loose the individual Protestant regarding matters of doctrine and morals and scriptural interpretation. No, sir. If I, as a Protestant, have a different interpretation of a particular passage or set of passages in the Bible than my pastor does, then as a Protestant, I generally do not recognize him to have any sort of binding authority on me regarding his particular interpretation of Scripture versus my particular interpretation of Scripture. He has no authority to impose his interpretation on me, no authority to "bind" his interpretation on me, and no authority to overrule my individual interpretation of Scripture. He is entitled to his private fallible interpretations of Scripture, and I am entitled to my private fallible interpretations of Scripture. Which is why we have tens of thousands upon tens of thousands of Protestant denominations.

The question then becomes: Why did Jesus give His Church the power to bind and loose if, since the apostles, no one in His Church can exercise that authority?

This is why binding and loosing is a problem with Protestantism.

4

There Is No Protestant Catechism (Part 1)

If you ask a Catholic, "What does the Catholic Church teach on ..."
And then name any particular topic, the Catholic can reply, "Well,
you just need to look in the *Catechism of the Catholic Church* for the
answer to that."

If you ask a Protestant, "What does the Protestant Church teach on
..." and then name any particular topic, the Protestant cannot reply,
"Well, you just need to look in the *Catechism of the Protestant Church* for
the answer to that." They can't say that because there is no such thing
as a Protestant catechism. There is no one source within Protestantism
that a Catholic can consult to find out what Protestants believe on
any given article of faith or morals. But why is that a problem with
Protestantism?

It's a problem because of what Paul said to Timothy: "Remain at
Ephesus that you may charge certain persons not to teach any different
doctrine" (1 Tim. 1:3). Paul told Timothy to tell certain people "not to
teach any different doctrine."

There is no such thing as a *Catechism of the Protestant Church* because
people teach "different doctrine" all over the place. For instance, some
Protestant denominations teach that infant Baptism is okay. Others
say it's not. Some say Baptism is regenerative (that through Baptism
one is "born again"). Others say it's merely symbolic. Some denominations teach the Rapture. Some don't. Some teach a pre-tribulation
Rapture. Others teach a mid-tribulation Rapture. Still others teach

a post-tribulation Rapture. Some denominations teach Once Saved, Always Saved. Others deny Once Saved, Always Saved. There are those denominations that teach salvation by faith alone. There are those denominations that don't. There are denominations that have priests. There are denominations that don't. There are denominations that have bishops. There are denominations that don't. There are denominations that have sacraments. There are denominations that don't. There are denominations that teach men can marry men and women can marry women. There are denominations that say marriage is between one man and one woman. There are denominations that worship on Saturday. There are denominations that worship on Sunday. Certain denominations allow divorce and remarriage. Certain denominations don't. A number of denominations say abortion is okay. A number of denominations say it's not. The Bible is inerrant. The Bible is not inerrant. God is Father. No, God is Mother. God is three Persons but one God. No, God is one Person but is known by three different names.

I could go on and on with pretty much any and every doctrine and dogma of any given Protestant denomination. So, you cannot have a *Catechism of the Protestant Church*, because on any given topic that would be discussed in a theoretical Protestant catechism, you would have a minimum of two different teachings, and possibly several different teachings. In other words, there is no teaching on faith and morals that you can say is universal throughout Protestantism, with the possible exception of *Sola Scriptura*—the Bible alone as the sole rule of faith. Although, there are different interpretations of even that fundamental dogma of Protestant teaching. For example, is the Bible the "sole" authority or the "sole infallible" authority when it comes to questions of faith and morals? It depends on which Protestant you ask.

The fact that there is no such thing as a Protestant catechism is directly related to the fact that people teach "different doctrine" all over the place within Protestantism. How can that be okay? How do Protestants live with that fact? Well, they will tell you, "Yes, there are differences in doctrine, but those differences are in the 'nonessential' doctrines, not in the 'essential' doctrines." Well, that's delusional at best and deceitful at worst. Wouldn't the Trinity be an "essential" doctrine? Yet there are those who have accepted Jesus Christ into their hearts as their personal Lord and Savior (i.e., they are "saved" Christians) who don't believe in the Trinity! If Baptism is regenerative, then wouldn't infant Baptism be an "essential" doctrine (unless one is born again of water and the Spirit, he cannot enter the Kingdom of God, according to John 3:3)? Yet Protestants are divided on infant baptism. So, not only are Protestants divided on many, if not all, of the so-called essential doctrines, but they are even divided on what one should really consider an essential doctrine.

Regardless of all this, the problem for Protestants is that Paul told Timothy to tell these other folks not to teach *any* different doctrine. *Any!* Let's think about this: Did Jesus teach any different doctrines to Peter than He taught to James and John? When the Holy Spirit guided the apostles into "all the truth" (John 16:13), did He guide Bartholomew to any different doctrinal truths than He guided Philip? When the Holy Spirit brought to the apostles remembrance of all that Jesus had told them (John 14:26), did He cause Jude to remember any different doctrinal teachings than He caused Thomas to remember? Did Paul maybe really mean to tell Timothy to charge certain persons not to teach any different *essential* doctrines?

No, no, no, and no! Jesus did not teach different doctrines to different apostles—*any* different doctrine. The apostles, having been taught by Jesus and enlightened and guided by the Holy Spirit, did not teach different doctrines to their disciples—*any* different doctrine. Paul, under the inspiration of the Holy Spirit, commanded Timothy, his disciple, to prevent other disciples from teaching different doctrines—*any* different doctrine. Paul, again under the inspiration of the Holy Spirit, taught Titus, his disciple, that any men Titus would ordain as bishops "must hold firm to the sure word as taught, so that [they] may be able to give instruction in sound doctrine and also to confute those who contradict it" (Titus 1:9). Hold firm. Sure word. As taught. Sound doctrine. Confute those who contradict the sound doctrine. There is

33

no room here for teaching "any different doctrine." There is nothing here about it being okay to disagree on the "nonessentials" as long as you agree on the "essentials."

In fact, this whole thing about it being okay to disagree on the non-essentials is a crock. Jesus said if you can be trusted in the small things, then you can be trusted in the bigger things (see Luke 16:10; Matt. 25:21), which means that if you can't be trusted in the small things, then you can't be trusted in the bigger things. So, to acknowledge that you can't be trusted in the small things — that you could be wrong in the "nonessentials" — but then claim that you can indeed be absolutely trusted to get it right when it comes to the bigger things — the "essentials" — is the exact opposite of what Jesus teaches! If you can't get the small things right, then how can you be trusted in the bigger things?

So, knowing that neither Jesus nor the Holy Spirit taught different doctrines to the apostles and other disciples, and knowing that the apostles, who were guided by the Holy Spirit, did not teach different doctrines to their disciples and converts, and knowing that the apostles saw to it — as Paul's example shows us — that their disciples did not teach different doctrines to the next generation of disciples, then why is it that teaching different doctrines within different denominations is all hunky-dory within Protestantism? Hmmm ... good question.

All of this is why not having a Protestant catechism is a problem with Protestantism. Now, let me address two objections I've received in the past when I've asked people about the fact that there is no such thing as a Protestant catechism:

1. Yes, they say, there is such a thing as a Protestant catechism. For example, there are various "confessions" within Protestantism that are, essentially, catechisms.

2. There are, Protestants will claim, just as many divisions and different beliefs in Catholicism, so you can't really say Catholics have a unity of belief that is reflected in the *Catechism of the Catholic Church*.

To the former argument, I say this: The very fact that I am referred to several different confessions of faith (or catechisms) when I make the argument that there is no Protestant equivalent to the *Catechism of the Catholic Church* is proof of my argument. As I stated earlier, there is not one source within Protestantism that a Catholic can consult to find out what Protestants believe on any given article of faith or morals. This is not true of Catholicism. Furthermore, the confessions of faith that I am often referred to — such as the Thirty-nine Articles (Anglican, 1563); Belgic Confession (Christian Reformed, 1561), Augsburg Confession (Lutheran, 1530), Baptist Confession (Baptist, 1689), Westminster Confession (Methodist, 1646), and others — all conflict with one another in one or more areas, further proving my point. Those confessions may be good for their particular denomination (although many of the articles within those confessions are no longer believed by even those particular denominations), but they are not universally held within Protestantism. (For more on this, see below.)

To the latter argument, I say this: There is one body of teaching in the Catholic Church. One and *only* one. If there are folks who call themselves Catholic but who do not agree with one or more doctrines and dogmas of the Church, then these people are known as dissenters. They are, in essence, Protestants. They are no longer one with the Church. The body of doctrine and dogmas of the Church, however, is one. In Protestantism, is there one set body of doctrine and dogmas? No, there is not. In Protestantism, you have a myriad of beliefs (all supposedly from the same Bible) spanning a myriad of denominations, and it is a perfectly acceptable situation for most Protestants to have all of these varying beliefs.

One is not a dissenter or a heretic in Protestantism; one merely starts a new denomination, and then their different belief (or beliefs) is accepted as normal — at least for that denomination. So, yes, there are dissenters to Catholic teaching within the Church, and they may indeed try to pass off as "Catholic" the dissent that they teach, but it has no official stamp of approval from anyone. There is an authoritative body within the Catholic Church (the pope and the Magisterium) that is recognized as such by Catholics and non-Catholics alike, which gives witness to only one set of official and authoritative beliefs in Catholicism—the set of beliefs found in the *Catechism of the Catholic Church*. Protestantism has nothing like this.

In closing, I will repeat what I said in issue 255 of *Apologetics for the Masses*:

> Regarding the Protestant catechisms you mention, do you really wish to contend that they are similar to the *Catechism of the Catholic Church*? Really?! The *Catechism of the Catholic Church* is a systematic and detailed explanation of the Catholic Faith. If someone reads that, they will know the official teaching of the Catholic Church. Which catechism can I read that gives me the official teachings of Protestantism in its entirety? Is the Reformed catechism the official teaching of the Baptists? Is the Baptist catechism thefficeial teaching of the Methodist Church? And what about all of those nondenominational denominations out there? Where are the catechisms with their official teachings? Which of the Protestant catechisms that you know of represent the official teaching of all of Protestantism? Sorry, but there is no source book a Catholic can go to in order to find the official teaching of all of Protestantism. That book does not exist. Whereas, there is a source book that Protestants can go to in order to find the official teaching of all Catholics.

All of that is to say that the nonexistence of a *Catechism of the Protestant Church* is a significant issue for Protestants because it highlights the fact that there is no one, official, authoritative set of beliefs in Protestantism; yet the Bible clearly shows us there was one, official, authoritative set of beliefs in the early Church—the Church that Jesus founded. And there still is today one, official, authoritative set of beliefs in the Catholic Church—the Church that Jesus founded.

So, the fact that there is no Protestant catechism is a problem with Protestantism.

5

There Is No Protestant Catechism (Part 2)

Does Protestantism have a functional equivalent to the *Catechism of the Catholic Church* — a book that any Catholic can pick up to figure out, without a whole lot of difficulty, what is the Protestant belief on this or that topic of faith? For example, is there a Protestant catechism that lays out exactly what Protestant beliefs are regarding *Sola Scriptura* or *Sola Fide* or the Rapture or Once Saved, Always Saved or a whole host of other doctrinal issues that Catholics and Protestants differ on? As I argued in the last chapter, the answer to that question is: "No, there is not."

Protestants will say that there is such a thing as a Protestant catechism. They will tell you that a number of denominations have a catechism. But that's just it — there are Protestant catechisms, plural. Different Protestant denominations have their own particular catechism. However, there is not one overarching catechism that lays out all of the various Protestant teachings from all the tens of thousands, if not hundreds of thousands, of Protestant denominations. And the Protestant denominational catechisms that do exist are pretty much useless to someone interested in finding out what Protestants, in general, believe regarding any particular doctrine or dogma.

And the reason I say that is because I've tried. My comments are based on my reading of a number of Protestant catechisms and confessions of faith, which I will cite below, that were generally all over the map regarding what Protestantism teaches on this or that topic.

(The portions of most of the catechisms and confessions that I cite are written out in the reference section below my comments if you would like to see the exact quotes.)

Let's begin with the man who started it all for the Protestants: Martin Luther. Luther wrote something known as the *Small Catechism* because it was rather short, since it was aimed at young people and those that are pretty much ignorant of the Christian faith. Given the target audience, it just contained the basics—the Commandments, the Creed, the Our Father, the sacraments, and a few other things. It was literally a small catechism.

So, what does the *Small Catechism* have to say? In section 1 of *Luther's Small Catechism*, he lists the Ten Commandments. The first commandment is: "Thou shalt have no other gods." And of course we all know that for Protestants, the second commandment is: "Thou shalt not make unto thee any graven images," right? Oops, not quite right. At least, not according to *Luther's Small Catechism*. The second commandment, according to Martin Luther, the founder of Protestantism, is as follows: "Thou shalt not take the name of the Lord, thy God, in vain." Wow, it's the exact same as the second commandment in the list the Catholics use. So, if anyone ever tells you again that the Catholic Church changed the Ten Commandments so that we could drop the one about "graven images," just ask them if they would accept the testimony of Martin Luther on the matter. Then tell them what the second commandment is, at least according to Martin Luther.

Luther does, however, do something different with the Ten Commandments that I haven't seen anywhere else. His ninth commandment is: "Thou shalt not covet thy neighbor's house," and the tenth commandment is: "Thou shalt not covet thy neighbor's wife, nor his man-servant, nor his maid-servant, nor his cattle, nor anything that is his." So, the neighbor's house is apparently more important to single out than his wife. But the point is, he still breaks up the tenth commandment of most Protestants—"Thou shalt not covet"—into two separate commandments, just like the Catholics do.

However, in the *Heidelberg Catechism* of 1563, put forth by Reformed Protestantism (Calvinists), the second commandment is listed as: "Thou shalt not make unto thee any graven image." We see the same thing in the Reformed Westminster *Shorter Catechism* of 1648 in Question 49C and in the *Baptist Catechism* of 1689 in Question 55.

So, which Protestant catechism can a Catholic pick up in order to know the definitive Protestant formulation of the Ten Commandments?

Also, in *Luther's Small Catechism*, we see that through Baptism, we receive the forgiveness of sins and eternal salvation (section IV). And in the Augsburg Confession, which is Lutheran, we see that Baptism is necessary for eternal salvation and that infants should be baptized (article IXC). Hmmm ... those sound pretty Catholic, don't they? The Calvinists, in their 1561 Belgic Confession, teach that through Baptism, one receives the Holy Spirit, the remission of sins, and is "received into God's Church" (article 34C). And this is confirmed in the Reformed Heidelberg Catechism (1563) in Questions 71, 72, and 74.

But in the *Baptist Catechism* of 1689, Baptism is considered to be an ordinance, not a sacrament as believed by the Lutherans and the Calvinists, and Baptism is considered to be merely symbolic — no washing away of sin, no Holy Spirit, no admittance into God's Church because of it (Question 97). Furthermore, infants are not to be baptized (Question 99). And the *Methodist Missions Catechism* of 1853 also tells us, in chapter XII, that Baptism is symbolic, but then it also says we should baptize infants.

So, which Protestant catechism can a Catholic pick up to find the definitive Protestant teaching on whether Baptism is a sacrament or an ordinance? Whether Baptism washes away sin, imbues the Holy Spirit, and makes one a member of the Body of Christ — the Church — or is merely symbolic? Whether babies should be baptized or not?

Back to *Luther's Small Catechism*. In it, we see that the Lutherans profess that Confession is a sacrament and that by confessing your sins to a confessor, a mere man, one can receive absolution of his sins from his confessor (Section V). We see this mentioned again in Article XI of the Augsburg Confession (Lutheran). But there is absolutely no mention of Confession as a sacrament or even as an ordinance in any of the Reformed catechisms and confessions. Nor in the Baptist, nor the Methodist, nor the Presbyterian.

So, which Protestant catechism can a Catholic pick up to find the definitive Protestant teaching on Confession? Is it a sacrament or not? Can the confessor absolve you of your sins or not?

Now, what do Protestant catechisms say regarding the Eucharist, or the Lord's Supper, or simply "the Sacrament," as the Lutherans refer to it in their early documents? In Section VI of the *Small Catechism*, Luther states that the Eucharist is truly the Body and Blood of Christ under the bread and wine. The Augsburg Confession teaches the same in Article X. However, the *Heidelberg Catechism* states that the Eucharist is merely symbolic (Question 78). The *Baptist Catechism* of 1689 makes an even stronger statement about the symbolic nature of the Eucharist.

So, which Protestant catechism can a Catholic pick up to find the definitive Protestant teaching on the Eucharist (the Lord's Supper)? Is it really the Body and Blood of Christ, or merely a symbolic representation thereof? Is it a sacrament or an ordinance?

Now let's look at this teaching regarding Eternal Security, or Once Saved, Always Saved. What is the teaching of Protestantism on that? There is no mention of it in the *Small Catechism* or in the Augsburg Confession. Rather curious, don't you think? In the *Heidelberg Catechism*, which, again, is Calvinist, it says that the Kingdom of Heaven can be open and shut through Church discipline—sort of an excommunication type of thing—so there's no Eternal Security in Calvinism (Question 85). Or is there? In the Canons of Dort (1618), which is also Reformed Protestantism, Articles 12 and 13 say there is assurance of salvation, that the believer's election cannot be revoked. But the *Methodist Missions Catechism* says, in chapter IX, that one can lose their salvation through sin.

So, which Protestant catechism can a Catholic pick up to find the definitive Protestant teaching on Eternal Security (Once Saved, Always Saved) or even the definitive Calvinist teaching on it?

And which Protestant catechism can a Catholic pick up to find the definitive Protestant teaching on the Rapture? It's not mentioned anywhere in *Luther's Small Catechism*, or the Augsburg Confession, or the Belgic Confession, or the *Heidelberg Catechism*, or the Canons of Dort, or the Westminster *Shorter Catechism*, or the *Baptist Catechism*, or the *Methodist Missions Catechism*, or the *Methodist Episcopal Catechism* (1853), or the *Presbyterian Intermediate Catechism* (1912). In fact, the *Baptist Catechism*, Question 40, states that the bodies of believers who die rest in their graves until the resurrection, not until the Rapture! Which Protestant catechism or confession of faith is the Rapture in?

Another thing I wish to make note of: I have had, on several occasions, various Protestant apologists tell me that I am wrong when I define *Sola Scriptura* as the belief that the Bible is the sole rule of faith for Protestants—that everything the Christian needs to believe about his faith is found in the Bible. "Oh no," they say, "it's not the *sole* rule of faith, it's simply the sole *infallible* rule of faith." Well, let's take a few quotes about the Bible from some of these catechisms and confessions.

Belgic Confession, Article 7: "We believe that this Holy Scripture contains the will of God completely and that everything one must believe to be saved is sufficiently taught in it."

Baptist Catechism, Question 4: "The holy scriptures of the Old and New Testament are the word of God, and the only certain rule of faith and obedience."

Catechism of the Methodist Episcopal Church, Question 76: "All correct knowledge of religious truth and duty" is contained in the Bible.

In the same catechism, Question 78: The Bible is "the only sufficient rule of a Christian's faith and practice."

"Completely," "everything," "only," and "all"—there is nothing in any of these statements that makes a distinction between Scripture being the sole or only rule of faith versus it being the only "infallible" rule of faith or that there are even fallible rules of faith out there.

Something else I found very interesting: In *Luther's Small Catechism*, in the section on Daily Prayers, he talks about how, when you pray, you should make the Sign of the Cross. How many Protestants do that today?

Also, in the Westminster *Shorter Catechism*, Question 25 talks about how Christ makes "continual intercession for us." And it does so in the context of Christ as priest and dying for us on the Cross. If His death on the Cross was "once for all," then why does He need to make "continual intercession for us"? Catholics are often criticized for saying Mass over and over and over again. "Don't you know He died once for us and that there is no need for anything else?" But Hebrews 7:25 talks about Him interceding for us. Well, what is He offering on our behalf as He intercedes for us? He is re-presenting to the Father His offering of Himself on the Cross—which is the offering that we participate in, and re-present, at every Mass. If Christ is doing it, why shouldn't we also be doing it? The Reformed folks understand that, or at least they did once.

Another thing in the Westminster *Shorter Catechism* that I found exceedingly interesting is in Question 37. It says that the souls of believers are "made perfect" at death. Hmm ... what does that sound like? You mean, believers who die, yet their souls are not yet perfect, are somehow, through some process, purged of those imperfections in their souls before they make it into Heaven? I think there is a Catholic word for that, but I'm not really sure what it is. What is that word? I think it starts with a *P*. And the exact same teaching is found in Question 40 of the *Baptist Catechism*! What is that word?

Finally, in the Protestant Reformed Churches in America's "Declaration of Principles" (1951), the very first article says this: "They repudiate the errors of the Three Points adopted by the Synod of the Christian Reformed Church of Kalamazoo, 1924."

So, which of those statements of faith is more authoritative, the one issued by the Christian Reformed Church of Kalamazoo in 1924 or the Protestant Reformed Churches in America's "Declaration of Principles" of 1951 that repudiates the 1924 statement? Which of those two confessions of faith can a Catholic pick up to find the definitive Protestant teaching in the matter these folks were disagreeing about?

All of that is simply to point out that there is no document in all of Protestantism that functions in the same way the *Catechism of the Catholic Church* does. There is no one source that a Catholic can turn to in order to know the definitive Protestant teaching on this or that doctrine of faith and morals. It does not exist. But why do you think that is? I'll tell you why. It's because within Protestantism, there are tens of thousands upon tens of thousands of "authorities," each declaring what is and is not authentic Christian teaching and practice and each interpreting the Bible in their own way. However, no Protestant has the authority to bind any other Protestant in what he believes. It's a system that just doesn't work. It's a system that results in doctrinal and moral chaos. It's a system that flies in the face of Scripture's admonition "Not to teach any different doctrine" (1 Tim. 1:3).

It is a problem with Protestantism.

Reference Material

THE SMALL CATECHISM — MARTIN LUTHER (1529)
Section I: The Ten Commandments

(I'm not going to list them all here, just the first, second, ninth, and tenth.)

- First commandment: "Thou shalt have no other gods."

- Second commandment: "Thou shalt not take the name of the Lord, thy God, in vain."

- Ninth commandment: "Thou shalt not covet thy neighbor's house."

- Tenth commandment: "Thou shalt not covet thy neighbor's wife, nor his man-servant, nor his maid-servant, nor his cattle, nor anything that is his."

Section IV: The Sacrament of Holy Baptism

"It works forgiveness of sins, delivers from death and the devil, and gives eternal salvation to all who believe this, as the words and promises of God declare."

"It is not the water indeed that does them, but the word of God which is in and with the water, and faith, which trusts such word of God in the water. For without the word of God the water is simple water and no baptism. But with the word of God it is a baptism, that is, a gracious water of life and a washing of regeneration in the Holy Ghost, as St. Paul says, Titus, chapter three:

> 'By the washing of regeneration and renewing of the Holy Ghost, which He shed on us abundantly through Jesus Christ, our Savior, that, being justified by His grace, we should be made heirs according to the hope of eternal life. This is a faithful saying.'"

"It signifies that the old Adam in us should, by daily contrition and repentance, be drowned and die with all sins and evil lusts, and, again, a new man daily come forth and arise; who shall live before God in righteousness and purity forever."

Section V: Confession

"Confession embraces two parts: the one is, that we confess our sins; the other, that we receive absolution, or forgiveness, from the confessor, as from God Himself, and in no wise doubt, but firmly believe, that our sins are thereby forgiven before God in heaven."

"You should speak to the confessor thus: Reverend and dear sir, I beseech you to hear my confession, and to pronounce forgiveness to me for God's sake."

"And by the command of our Lord Jesus Christ I forgive thee thy sins, in the name of the Father and of the Son and of the Holy Ghost. Amen. Depart in peace."

Section VI: The Sacrament of the Altar [the Eucharist]

"It is the true body and blood of our Lord Jesus Christ, under the bread and wine, for us Christians to eat and to drink, instituted by Christ Himself."

THE AUGSBURG CONFESSION — LUTHERAN (1530)

Article VIII: What the Church Is

"Both the Sacraments and Word are effectual by reason of the institution and commandment of Christ, notwithstanding they be administered by evil men."

Article IX: Baptism

"Of Baptism they teach that it is necessary to salvation, and that through Baptism is offered the grace of God, and that children are to be baptized who, being offered to God through Baptism are received into God's grace."

"They condemn the Anabaptists, who reject the baptism of children, and say that children are saved without Baptism."

Article X: Of the Lord's Supper

"Of the Supper of the Lord they teach that the Body and Blood of Christ are truly present, and are distributed to those who eat the Supper of the Lord; and they reject those that teach otherwise."

Article XI: Confession

"Of Confession they teach that Private Absolution ought to be retained in the churches."

Article XII: Of Repentance

"Of Repentance they teach that for those who have fallen after Baptism there is remission of sins whenever they are converted and that the Church ought to impart absolution to those thus returning to repentance."

Article XVII: Of Christ's Return to Judgment

"Also they teach that at the Consummation of the World Christ will appear for judgment, and will raise up all the dead; He will give to the godly and elect eternal life and everlasting joys, but ungodly men and the devils He will condemn to be tormented without end."

"They condemn also others who are now spreading certain Jewish opinions, that before the resurrection of the dead the godly shall take possession of the kingdom of the world, the ungodly being everywhere suppressed."

THE BELGIC CONFESSION — REFORMED CONFESSION OF FAITH (1561)

Article 7: The Sufficiency of Scripture

"We believe that this Holy Scripture contains the will of God completely and that everything one must believe to be saved is sufficiently taught in it."

Article 15: The Doctrine of Original Sin

"It is a corruption of the whole human nature—an inherited depravity which even infects small infants in their mother's womb, and the root which produces in humanity every sort of sin. It is therefore so vile and enormous in God's sight that it is enough to condemn the human race, and it is not abolished or wholly uprooted even by baptism."

Article 33: The Sacraments

"There are only two: the sacrament of baptism and the Holy Supper of Jesus Christ."

Article 34: Baptism

"Having abolished circumcision, which was done with blood, Christ established in its place the sacrament of baptism. By it we are received into God's church."

"In this way God signifies to us that just as water washes away the dirt of the body when it is poured on us and also is seen on the bodies of those who are baptized when it is sprinkled on them."

"It [baptism] washes and cleanses it [the soul] from its sins and transforms us from being the children of wrath into the children of God."

"For that reason we reject the error of the Anabaptists who are not content with a single baptism once received and also condemn the baptism of the children of believers. We believe our children ought to be baptized and sealed with the sign of the covenant, as little children were circumcised in Israel on the basis of the same promises made to our children."

"Furthermore, baptism does for our children what circumcision did for the Jewish people. That is why Paul calls baptism the 'circumcision of Christ' (Col 2:11)."

Article 37: The Last Judgment

"Finally we believe, according to God's Word, that when the time appointed by the Lord is come (which is unknown to all creatures) and the number of the elect is complete, our Lord Jesus Christ will come from heaven, bodily and visibly, as he ascended, with great glory and majesty, to declare himself the judge of the living and the dead. He will burn this old world, in fire and flame, in order to cleanse it. Then all human creatures will appear in person before the great judge.... They will be summoned there 'with the archangel's call and with the sound of God's trumpet' (1 Thes 4:16). For all those who died before that time will be raised from the earth, their spirits being joined and united with their own bodies in which they lived. And as for those who are still alive, they will not die like the others but will be changed 'in the twinkling of an eye' from perishable to imperishable (1 Cor 15:51–53). Then the books (that is, the consciences) will be opened, and the dead will be judged according to the things they did in the world (Rv 20:12), whether good or evil."

Heidelberg Catechism — Reformed (1563)

Question 71: Where has Christ promised that we are as certainly washed with his blood and Spirit as with the water of baptism?

"In the institution of Baptism, which runs thus: Go ye, therefore, and teach all nations, baptizing them in the name of the Father, and of the Son, and of the Holy Ghost (Mt 28:19). He that believeth and is baptized, shall be saved; but he that believeth not, shall be damned (Mk 16:16). This promise is also repeated, where the Scripture calls Baptism the washing of regeneration (Ti 3:5) and the washing away of sins (Acts 22:16)."

Question 72: "Is, then, the outward washing with water itself the washing away of sins?

"No (Mt 3:11; 1 Pt 3:21; Eph 5:26–27); for only the blood of Jesus Christ and the Holy Ghost cleanse us from all sin (1 Jn 1:7; 1 Cor 6:11)."

Question 74: Are infants also to be baptized?

"Yes; for since they, as well as their parents, belong to the covenant and people of God (Gn 17:7; 1 Cor 7:14; Jl 2:16; Mt 19:14), and both redemption from sin and the Holy Ghost, who works faith, are through the blood of Christ promised to them no less than to their parents (Lk 1:14–15; Ps 22:10; Is 44:1–3; Acts 2:39, 16:31), they are also by baptism, as a sign of the covenant, to be ingrafted into the Christian Church, and distinguished from the children of unbelievers (Acts 10:47; 1 Cor 12:13; 2 Cor 6:15), as was done in the Old Testament by Circumcision (Gn 17:12–14), in place of which in the New Testament Baptism is appointed (Col 2:11–13)."

Question 76: What is it to eat the crucified body and drink the shed blood of Christ?

"It is not only to embrace with a believing heart all the sufferings and death of Christ, and thereby to obtain the forgiveness of sins and life eternal (1 Cor 10:16; Jn 6:35, 40, 48, 50–51, 53–54), but moreover, also, to be so united more and more to his sacred body by the Holy

Ghost, who dwells both in Christ and in us (Jn 6:55–56; 1 Cor 12:13), that although he is in heaven (Acts 3:21, 1:9–11; 1 Cor 11:26; Col 3:1), and we on earth, we are nevertheless flesh of his flesh and bone of his bones (Eph 3:16–17, 5:30; 1 Cor 6:15–19; 1 Jn 3:24, 4:13), and live and are governed forever by one Spirit, as members of the same body are by one soul (Jn 14:23, 6:47, 57–58, 15:1–6; Eph 4:15–16)."

Question 78: Do, then, the bread and wine become the real body and blood of Christ?

"No; but as the water in Baptism is not changed into the blood of Christ, nor becomes the washing away of sins itself, being only the divine token and assurance thereof (Mt 26:29; Mk 14:24; Jn 6:35–63; Eph 5:26; Acts 22:16), so also in the Lord's Supper the sacred bread does not become the body of Christ itself (1 Cor 10:16–17, 11:26–28), though agreeably to the nature and usage of sacraments (Gn 17:10–11; Ex 12:26–27, 43, 48, 13:9; Acts 7:8; Ex 24:8; Lv 16:10, 17:11; Is 6:6–7; Ti 3:5; Acts 22:16; 1 Pt 3:21; 1 Cor 10:1–4) it is called the body of Christ."

Question 85: How is the kingdom of heaven shut and opened by Church discipline?

"In this way: that, according to the command of Christ, if any under the Christian name show themselves unsound either in doctrine or life, and after repeated brotherly admonition refuse to turn from their errors or evil ways, they are complained of to the Church or to its proper officers (Rom 12:7–9; 1 Cor 12:28; 1 Tm 5:17), and, if they neglect to hear them also, are by them excluded from the holy Sacraments and the Christian communion, and by God himself from the kingdom of Christ (Mt 18:15–18; 1 Cor 5:3–5; 2 Thes 3:14–15; 2 John 10–11); and if they promise and show real amendment, they are again received as members of Christ and his Church (Lk 15:20–24; 2 Cor 2:5–8, 10)."

Question 92: What is the law of God?

"God spake all these words, saying (Ex 20:1–17; Dt 5:5–21):

Second Commandment: Thou shalt not make unto thee any graven image, or any likeness of any thing that is in heaven above, or that is in the earth beneath, or that is in the water under the earth; thou shalt not bow down thyself to them, nor serve them. For I the Lord thy God am a jealous God, visiting the iniquity of the fathers upon the children unto the third and fourth generation of them that hate me; and shewing mercy unto thousands of them that love me and keep my commandments (Ex 20:4–6; Dt 5:8–10)."

Canons of Dort — Reformed (1619)

Article 12: The Assurance of Election

"Assurance of their eternal and unchangeable election to salvation is given to the chosen in due time, though by various stages and in differing measure. Such assurance comes not by inquisitive searching into the hidden and deep things of God, but by noticing within themselves, with spiritual joy and holy delight, the unmistakable fruits of election pointed out in God's Word—such as a true faith in Christ, a childlike fear of God, a godly sorrow for their sins, a hunger and thirst for righteousness, and so on."

Article 13: The Fruit of This Assurance

"In their awareness and assurance of this election, God's children daily find greater cause to humble themselves before God, to adore the fathomless depth of God's mercies, to cleanse themselves, and to give fervent love in return to the One who first so greatly loved them. This is far from saying that this teaching concerning election, and reflection upon it, make God's children lax in observing his commandments or carnally self-assured. By God's just judgment this does usually happen to those who casually take for granted the grace of election or engage in idle and brazen talk about it but are unwilling to walk in the ways of the chosen."

Article 17: The Salvation of the Infants of Believers

"Since we must make judgments about God's will from his Word, which testifies that the children of believers are holy, not by nature but by virtue of the gracious covenant in which they together with their parents are included, godly parents ought not to doubt the election and salvation of their children whom God calls out of this life in infancy."

WESTMINSTER SHORTER CATECHISM — REFORMED (1648)

Question 25: How doth Christ execute the office of a priest?

"Christ executeth the office of a priest, in his once offering up of himself a sacrifice to satisfy divine justice, and reconcile us to God; and in making continual intercession for us."

Question 37: What benefits do believers receive from Christ at death?

"The souls of believers are at their death made perfect in holiness, and do immediately pass into glory; and their bodies, being still united to Christ, do rest in their graves till the resurrection."

Question 49: Which is the second commandment?

"The second commandment is, Thou shalt not make unto thee any graven image."

Question 94: What is baptism?

"Baptism is a sacrament, wherein the washing with water, in the name of the Father, and of the Son, and of the Holy Ghost, doth signify and seal our ingrafting into Christ, and partaking of the benefits of the covenant of grace, and our engagement to be the Lord's."

Question 95: To whom is baptism to be administered?

"Baptism is not to be administered to any that are out of the visible church, till they profess their faith in Christ, and obedience to him; but the infants of such as are members of the visible church, are to be baptized."

Baptist Catechism (1689)

Question 4: What is the word of God?

"The holy scriptures of the Old and New Testament are the word of God, and the only certain rule of faith and obedience (2 Tm 3:16; Eph 2:20)."

Question 40: What benefits do believers receive from Christ at their death?

"The souls of believers are at their death made perfect in holiness (Heb 12:23), and do immediately pass into glory (2 Cor 5:1, 6, 8; Phil 1:23; Lk 23:43); and their bodies being still united to Christ (1 Thes 4:14), do rest in their graves (Is 57:2) till the resurrection (Job 19:26–27)."

Question 55: Which is the second commandment?

"The second commandment is, Thou shalt not make unto thee any graven image."

Question 97: What is baptism?

"Baptism is an ordinance of the New Testament instituted by Jesus Christ, to be unto the party baptized a sign of his fellowship with him, in his death, burial, and resurrection; of his being ingrafted into him (Rom 6:3–5; Col 2:12; Gal 3:27); of remission of sins (Mk 1:4; Acts 2:38, 22:16); and of his giving up himself unto God through Jesus Christ, to live and walk in newness of life (Rom 6:3–4)."

Question 99: Are the infants of such as are professing believers to be baptized?

"The infants of such as are professing believers are not to be baptized, because there is neither command or example in the holy scriptures, or certain consequence from them to baptize such (Ex 23:13; Prv 30:6; Lk 3:7–8)."

Question 102: What is the Lord's supper?

"The Lord's supper is an ordinance of the New Testament, instituted by Jesus Christ; wherein by giving and receiving bread and wine, according to his appointment, his death is shown forth, and the worthy receivers are, not after a corporal and carnal manner, but by faith, made partakers of his body and blood, with all his benefits, to their spiritual nourishment and growth in grace (Mt 26:26–28; 1 Cor 11:23–26, 10:16)."

METHODIST MISSIONS CATECHISM (1853)

Chapter VIII: The Judgment

[No mention of a Rapture. Quotes from the Rapture passage in Thessalonians but believes it to be referring to the end of time.]

Chapter IX: Who Are Righteous

"The righteous are those who believe the Gospel and live it."

"If our sins are forgiven and we get a new heart, can we fall away and lose it? Yes; Adam fell away and Judas fell away; and we can fall, too."

"How must we live so as not to fall from God's grace? We must deny ourself and take up our cross daily, and follow Jesus."

Chapter XII: The Sacraments

1. "What is baptism? Baptism is a sign of the grace of God that makes us Christians."

2. "Does Baptism make us Christians? No; water cannot make us Christians; grace makes us Christians."

4. "Ought little children to be baptized? Yes, they belong to Christ."

CATECHISM OF THE METHODIST EPISCOPAL CHURCH (1855)

71–72: [Baptism — washing of sin; regeneration; admittance to the Church.]

76: "All correct knowledge of religious truth and duty [is derived from the Bible]."

78: "The only sufficient rule of a Christian's faith and practice [is the Bible]."

89: Second Commandment: "Thou shalt not make unto thee any graven image."

PRESBYTERIAN INTERMEDIATE CATECHISM (1912)

18: Salvation by faith alone

33: Baptism is symbolic

34: Infant baptism

DECLARATION OF PRINCIPLES OF THE PROTESTANT REFORMED CHURCHES (1951)

I. "They repudiate the errors of the Three Points adopted by the Synod of the Christian Reformed Church of Kalamazoo, 1924."

6

Sin Has Consequences

The fact that sin has consequences is a problem with Protestantism because in *Sola Fide* Protestantism—Protestant faith traditions that believe we are saved by faith alone—when you actually examine what they are teaching, you realize that the logical consequence of the dogma of salvation by faith alone, and its corollary—Once Saved, Always Saved—is that sin has no consequences.

Think about it. We are saved by faith alone. As long as I have faith, as long as I have accepted Jesus Christ into my heart as my personal Lord and Savior, I'm saved. The only determinate of whether we go to Heaven or Hell is whether we have faith or not. Sin plays absolutely no role in the fate of our souls. Nonbelievers go to Hell. Why? Because they sinned? No! Because they didn't have faith. Believers don't go to Hell. Why? Because they were holy? No! Because they have faith. Regardless of the sins they commit, they still go to Heaven because they have faith.

The problem for Protestantism with all of this is that it goes against almost every grain of the Bible. For example, in Matthew 25, when Jesus is talking about the Last Judgment (vv. 31–46), what is it that separates the sheep (who inherit the Kingdom of Heaven) and the goats (who inherit Hell)? Do the sheep have faith and the goats don't? Nope. The sheep do things for others—feed the hungry, clothe the naked, and so on—and the goats don't. In other words, the goats commit sins of omission. They sin by not helping their fellow man. And their sins have consequences. They end up in Hell.

But according to *Sola Fide*, this ought not be so! Jesus should have said to the sheep on His right hand, "You accepted Me into your heart as your personal Lord and Savior; come, inherit the kingdom prepared for you." And He should have said to the goats, "You never accepted Me into your hearts as your personal Lord and Savior, so depart from Me into the eternal fire." But He didn't. He said one group had done right and the other group had sinned. And there was a consequence—an eternal consequence—for those that sinned (and of course, never repented of their sin). Sin has consequences.

In Revelation 21:8, we are told the following: "But as for the cowardly, the faithless, the polluted, as for murderers, fornicators, sorcerers, idolaters, and all liars, their lot shall be in the lake that burns with fire and brimstone, which is the second death." What do we see here? Well, we see people that the Word of God is telling us are headed to Hell, the "lake that burns with fire and brimstone ... the second death," because of their sins. Sin has consequences here. Furthermore, there is no distinction made here between believers and unbelievers. In fact, unbelief, being faithless, is cited as just one type of sin along with murder, fornication, sorcery, and others that will get you sent to Hell. The fact that unbelievers are specifically mentioned as just one type of sinner shows that this list is talking about believers and unbelievers alike. Nowhere does it say that this list is just referring to unbelievers.

In fact, in *Sola Fide* theology, it wouldn't make sense for this list to be referring to just unbelievers. If it was referring to unbelievers, then it should have just said, "But as for the faithless, their lot shall be in the lake that burns with fire and brimstone." Because it isn't murder or fornication or sorcery or idolatry or lying that gets one sent to Hell, it is unbelief—period! In *Sola Fide* theology, believers can commit all of those sins, and not repent of them, and still go to Heaven because it is by faith alone that you are saved.

In Romans 2:8, what does God render to those who are contentious and do not obey the truth but instead obey wickedness? The book says God will render to them wrath and fury. That's not talking about Heaven. Sin has consequences.

And there is literally passage after passage after passage in the New Testament that tells us sin has consequences. But let me wrap this up with one final passage. This passage in Matthew 5 shows beyond a shadow of a doubt that sin can, and does, have consequences—eternal consequences—for believers, contrary to what *Sola Fide* theology teaches. In verses 27–30, Jesus tells His listeners that if their right eye causes them to sin, pluck it out. Or if their right hand causes them to sin, cut it off. Why does He say that? He says it to stress in a very strong way the point that you need to avoid sin at all costs because sin will get you sent to Hell. And we know he was not talking about unbelievers here because if His listeners are able to avoid sin, then they will not go to Hell, which means they will go to Heaven. And for that to happen, Protestant theology says they have to be believers.

If *Sola Fide* is true, then there would be no reason for Jesus to tell these folks to pluck out their eye or cut off their hand to avoid sinning. There would be no reason because if He is talking to believers, then they are going to Heaven whether they sin or not, so why pluck out an eye or cut off a hand? That's so not necessary, Jesus. There would be no reason because if He is talking to unbelievers, then even if they pluck out their eyes or cut off their hands, they are still going to Hell because of their unbelief. If *Sola Fide* is true, then this passage of Scripture, along with many, many others, is completely bogus and nonsensical.

So, Jesus is telling *believers* here in Matthew 5:27–30 that if they sin, they could end up in Hell. Again, that is not possible in *Sola Fide* theology. In *Sola Fide* theology, believers go to Heaven. There's no need to pluck out an eye or cut off a hand. Their sins have no consequence in regard to their salvation. In the Bible, though, the Word of God tells us sin does indeed have consequences in regard to the salvation of believers.

To summarize: In the Bible, sin has consequences in regard to one's salvation. In the theology of the vast majority of Protestantism, however, sin does not have consequences when it comes to your salvation. You either believe or you don't believe. If you believe, you go to Heaven. If you don't believe, you go to Hell. So, which do you believe, the Bible or Protestant *Sola Fide* theology?

The fact that sin has consequences—eternal consequences—is a problem with Protestantism.

7

Jesus' Church Teaches Error

The Bible tells us that Jesus started a church. "And I tell you, you are Peter, and on this rock I will build my church" (Matt. 16:18). Not "churches." But "church." Singular. One. One church. Jesus mentions this church again, in Matthew 18:17, as the ultimate arbiter in disputes between a person and his brother. Or we could say, the ultimate arbiter in disputes between Christians, since it wouldn't be non-Christians seeking an authoritative decision from the Christian church.

The first leaders of this church Jesus founded were, without dispute, Peter and the apostles. At the Last Supper, Jesus tells these leaders of His church that He is going to send the Holy Spirit to them to "guide you into all the truth" (John 16:13). In Acts 15, we see confirmation in the letter sent out from the Council of Jerusalem that the Holy Spirit is indeed guiding not just the apostles but all the early leaders of the church gathered in council. The letter reads, in part, "For it has seemed good to the Holy Spirit and to us" (v. 28).

Jesus founded a church. He appointed the first leaders of this church. He sent the Holy Spirit to guide the leaders of this church. He gave the leaders of this church the mission to make disciples of all nations by baptizing them and by teaching them to observe all that He had commanded (Matt. 28:19–20). Jesus was given all authority in Heaven and on earth by the Father (Matt. 28:18), and He sent the leaders of this church out with that same authority (John 20:21).

Given all of that, would we expect the church founded by Jesus Christ and guided by the Holy Spirit to be capable of teaching error in matters of faith and morals? Of course not! Why would Jesus start a church that could teach error? How could it be said the Holy Spirit was guiding the church if the church could teach error? Can the Holy Spirit lead the church into error? The church, Scripture tells us, is the Body of Christ (Col. 1:24). It is one with its Head, Jesus Christ (Eph. 5:31–32). Does, then, the Bride of Christ, the church, teach error? Not if Jesus is God and if the Holy Spirit is God.

Furthermore, Jesus tells us that if we know the truth, the truth will make us free (John 8:32). He also said that He came to bear witness to the truth (John 18:37). How can we know the truth and be made free if the church He left behind, to teach us all that He commanded, is capable of teaching us error? How can He claim that He came to bear witness to the truth if the church He left behind to teach us can bear witness to error?

All of this leads into this chapter's problem with Protestantism, which is this: Protestantism, the Protestant church, taken as a whole or in its individual parts, teaches error. This is indisputable. I have never heard of a Protestant church that claims it doesn't teach error, nor have I ever come across a Protestant who doesn't acknowledge that his church teaches error. It is a phenomenon that I find absolutely fascinating. On the one hand, Protestants claim to be members of the church founded by Jesus Christ and guided by the Holy Spirit. Yet on the other hand, they readily admit that their church/denomination teaches error.

Of course, they will claim that any error their church teaches is error only in the "nonessential" doctrines. You know, those doctrines that are not necessary to believe for one's salvation. They might get the small stuff wrong, but they absolutely, beyond a shadow of a doubt, get the big stuff right. How does that work? If a math teacher gets the small stuff wrong—2 + 2, 5 x 5, the square root of 9—how can we be confident that he gets the big stuff right—matrix algebra, integral calculus, and Euclidean geometry, for example?

Jesus tells us in the Parable of the Talents that if He can trust you in the little things, then He can trust you in the bigger things. "Well done, good and faithful servant; you have been faithful over a little, I will set you over much" (Matt. 25:21). This strongly implies that if He can't trust you in the little things, then He sure as heck isn't going to trust you in the bigger things. So if you, as a church or denomination, aren't absolutely sure you're getting it right in the "nonessential" doctrines, how can you be absolutely sure you're getting it right in the "essential" doctrines? That makes no sense, whatsoever!

Someone might say, "But John, we're sure we get it right on the essentials because everyone agrees on those." I beg to differ. *Sola Fide*, salvation by faith alone, one of the two pillars of Protestantism (*Sola Scriptura* being the other), is agreed upon by the vast majority of Protestants. Yet there is a decent-sized minority of folks who don't agree with it. Another essential doctrine, Once Saved, Always Saved, is agreed upon by the majority of Protestants. Yet there is a significant minority who don't agree with it. The Trinity is another essential doctrine. Yet there are Protestants who don't believe in it.

In other words, you have disagreements among Protestants even on the so-called essential doctrines. Plus, you have disagreements over what is or is not an essential doctrine—Baptism, for example. If the Lutherans and Anglicans are right, and we are "born again," receive spiritual regeneration, through Baptism, which is necessary for our salvation, then that is an essential doctrine. If Baptists, Evangelicals, and non-denominationalists are right, and Baptism is merely a symbolic event that has no effect on our salvation, then it is a nonessential doctrine. Keeping the Commandments is essential for some (including Jesus; see Matt. 19:16–17), but nonessential for others.

So, no, not everyone agrees on the essential doctrines, and not everyone agrees on even what the essential doctrines within Protestantism are! Regardless, it still comes back to the fact that within Protestantism, no one church or group of churches or denomination claims to be absolutely correct in 100 percent of its doctrinal and moral teachings. Every single church that I know of gives itself a little leeway to be wrong on something. Why is that? As I explain elsewhere in this book, it's because of the lack of infallibility. If you don't have the charism, the gift, of infallibility in your church, then you cannot bind anyone to believe in anything you teach because anything you teach could, potentially, be wrong.

Another fascinating fact about all this is that every Protestant pastor in every Protestant church or denomination that denies infallibility, that denies he has the ability to teach doctrine and morals without error, that allows for the possibility that he could be teaching error (even if only in the "nonessential" doctrines), essentially admits that he is not in the church founded by Jesus Christ and guided by the Holy Spirit.

Again, Jesus taught without error. The Holy Spirit teaches without error. If your church could even theoretically be teaching error in faith and morals, then it cannot be the church founded by Jesus Christ, and it most definitely is not being guided by the Holy Spirit.

I want to sum all of this up by giving you a quote from a Protestant that I engaged with for several days on my Facebook page (John Martignoni and the Bible Christian Society), and then comment on what he said. I want to emphasize that I do not put this person forward as some sort of expert or authority on Protestantism. He's not. He's just an average Protestant who came onto my page to tell me how wrong the Catholic Church is in Her teachings. I'm just using what he says to drive home the point of this chapter.

Here's the quote: *"Well, scripturally, I believe ALL churches have at least SOME errors, though not always essentials. I've served in 7 churches and all did or taught SOME things differently."* (Words in all capitals in the original.)

A little analysis. First, where does Scripture say that "ALL churches have at least SOME errors"? It doesn't. Where does it say the church founded by Jesus Christ and guided by the Holy Spirit has at least "SOME" errors? It doesn't. To actually believe that Jesus founded, and the Holy Spirit guides, a church that teaches error is mind-boggling to me.

Note that this person said: "*I believe.*" Not to be rude, but who cares what he believes? This is all his opinion. His fallible, error-prone, non-authoritative, private opinion. And by what authority does he declare that "ALL churches have at least SOME errors"? Well, he declares it by the same authority every Protestant has: his own private interpretation of Scripture, which carries absolutely no authority whatsoever and which, by his own admission in other Facebook posts, is prone to error. Can someone say "faulty logic"?

Here's that logic in conversation form:

Person P: "*All* churches have at least *some* errors."

Person C: "Are you infallible?"

Person P: "No, of course not. No man is infallible."

Person C: "Then since you are not infallible, you could be wrong when you say that *all* churches have at least *some* errors."

Person P: "Yes, of course, I could be wrong."

Person C: "So, *all* churches might *not* have at least *some* errors, then."

Person P: "No, since no man is infallible, that means *all* churches have at least *some* errors."

Person C: "And that statement is based on your fallible interpretation of Scripture?"

Person P: "Absolutely."

"*All* churches have at least *some* errors." This means, then, as I've been saying, that *nothing* any church teaches can be trusted to be the truth. This, again, is the heart of the problem. I agree 100 percent with this guy's statement, as long as you confine the "ALL" to Protestant churches. As I say in other places in this book, this is the Achilles' heel of all Protestantism. In their reaction against Catholic teaching regarding the infallibility of the pope, they made it impossible, according to their own theology, for any believer in any Protestant church or in reading the Bible on his own to "know the truth" that will set him free (John 8:32) or to hear the voice of Jesus (John 18:37) with any degree of certainty.

If you admit that your church teaches error because there is no one in your church, or any church, who can interpret Scripture infallibly and who can teach infallibly, then you have essentially admitted that you have no way of knowing the truth. That's a *huge* problem!

"Though not always essentials." Again, what is essential and what is nonessential, and who decides? Does this guy on Facebook decide? Which error-prone church or individual decides this whole essential versus nonessential thing? Which Protestant church or churches, of which it is admitted they all teach at least some error, decides what is essential and what is nonessential? Is their decision infallible? And if all of your doctrines come straight from Scripture, then which part of Scripture are you calling "nonessential"? Which part of the Word of God is "nonessential"?

This guy served in seven churches from, apparently, seven different denominations since all of them did or taught some things differently. So, if you can't decide which one of them was right, what does that say about your ability to discern truth from error? It says you absolutely suck at it!

Here are my last words on this: The dirty little secret is that every Protestant who denies infallibility (which is pretty much every Protestant) is in the exact same boat as this guy I quoted from my Facebook page. If you deny infallibility, then you deny that there is any way to authoritatively settle disputes between Christians regarding matters of faith and morals. This means you deny anyone the ability to know, with certainty, what is true and what is false regarding Christian teaching. You have no rock to build your house upon, only the sand of your own fallible interpretations of the Bible.

Protestantism allows for error to be taught, in the areas of faith and morals, in the church founded by Jesus Christ and guided by the Holy Spirit. That simply makes no sense.

8

Korah's Rebellion

The Letter of Jude says this: "Woe to them! For they walk in the way of Cain, and abandon themselves for the sake of gain to Balaam's error, and perish in Korah's rebellion" (Jude 1:11). This verse is referring to those in the congregation Jude is writing to who "defile the flesh, reject authority, and revile the glorious ones" (v. 8). Other negative things are also said about these same people in verses 4, 12–13, and 15–16. But I want to focus specifically on what was said about them perishing in "Korah's rebellion."

What is that all about? Most people, if they ever bother to read Jude, just skim right over this verse and don't really stop to think about what it means. What this verse tells us is that there were people in the first few decades of the existence of Christianity who were perishing in something described as "Korah's rebellion."

What was Korah's rebellion? Numbers 16 tells us all about it. Korah was the son of Izhar, son of Kohath, son of Levi. He was a Levite. He instigated a rebellion of some of the Levites against Moses and Moses' brother, Aaron, who was the high priest. What was this rebellion all about? Well, it seems that Korah was not at all happy that Moses and Aaron, and Aaron's sons, had, in Korah's eyes, exalted themselves "above the assembly of the LORD" (v. 3). He further said in that same verse, "For all the congregation are holy, every one of them, and the LORD is among them."

Korah was upset that there was a ministerial priesthood that was set apart from the rest of the Israelites, particularly that it was set apart from the rest of the Levites. He was basically saying, "Who are you to think you have some sort of special role and authority? Don't you know that all of us are holy, and you have no business thinking that you can be priests of the Lord and we can't?" We can gather this from verses 8–10, when Moses says to Korah, "Hear now you sons of Levi: is it too small a thing for you that the God of Israel has separated you from the congregation of Israel, to bring you near to himself, to do service in the tabernacle of the LORD, and to stand before the congregation to minister to them; and that he has brought you near him, and all your brethren the sons of Levi with you?"

Moses is saying to him, "You are a Levite. You have been set apart to minister at the tabernacle of the Lord. And that isn't enough for you? You want more?" And what more did Korah want? The Word of God, in verse 10, tells us: "And would you seek the priesthood also?"

Korah was rebelling against the ministerial priesthood and the authority that goes with it. He was rebelling against Moses and, in particular, against the priesthood of Aaron and his sons. Korah was saying, "Hey, you're no different than us. We're holy just like you. You have no authority over us. We're all priests of God." And God punished Korah and those that joined him in his rebellion against the ministerial priesthood.

Now, bringing that back to the Letter of Jude, the vast majority of Protestant denominations and non-denominations do not believe in a ministerial priesthood. They believe in the priesthood of all believers (as do Catholics), but they do not believe in a ministerial or sacramental priesthood that is set apart from the rest of the "congregation" that has any special authority to do anything that all the believers can't do. They will rail against the Catholic priesthood and tell you that we are all priests and that there is no mention of a ministerial or sacramental priesthood in the New Testament.

These folks have told me, in no uncertain terms, that the priesthood, as the Catholic Church defines it and practices it, is a false teaching and a false practice since it's "not in the Bible." Yes, there is no direct mention of a ministerial priesthood in the New Testament that is definitively set apart from the rest of the people. However, there is indeed mention of those who are set apart for special service to the Lord and His people through the laying on of hands. Well, those are bishops, not priests, we are told. Okay, but at least admit that there are those who are set apart from the rest of the people by the laying on of hands, right? Also, as we see in Acts 6:3–6, some men were set apart for another type of special service to God and His people: the deacons. They had hands laid on them as well.

So, we see bishops and deacons having hands laid on them to be set apart from the rest of the people of God for special ministerial service that has a certain authority that goes along with it. But it doesn't say anything about priests, we are still told.

That's where Jude 1:11 comes in. There are people, the Word of God tells us, in the New Testament era who "perish in Korah's rebellion." They are perishing spiritually, not necessarily physically. Korah rebelled against "the priesthood" of Moses and Aaron and Aaron's sons, the Book of Numbers tells us, and he and those who followed him perished because of it—physically *and* spiritually. And it wasn't the priesthood of all believers he rebelled against. It was a ministerial priesthood made up of men who had been set apart from the people for special service to the Lord and who had been given special authority by God with which to carry out their duties.

So, if that's what Korah's rebellion was about, then how could Korah's rebellion be occurring in the New Testament era unless there was an ordained priesthood, a priesthood that reserved certain liturgical functions, certain acts of worship, for these men who were set apart to be priests? This passage from Jude makes absolutely no sense unless there was, from the earliest moments of the Church, an ordained priesthood. You can't have Korah's rebellion in first-century Christianity if there was no ordained priesthood, if there was no distinction between the royal priesthood of all believers and the ordained priesthood.

Jude could not be talking about people perishing in Korah's rebellion if there was no longer a separate and distinct priesthood. This means there was indeed a separate and distinct, an ordained, ministerial priesthood in early Christianity. In other words, the priesthood as the Catholic Church has it today—an ordained sacramental priest-hood—is in the Bible!

So, why is that a problem with Protestantism? Well, except for the Anglican and Lutheran Churches, I'm not aware of any other denominations within Protestantism that even claim to have a ministerial priesthood. Yet again, as Jude 1:11 shows us, there was indeed some sort of ministerial priesthood in the early Church. So, all of these *Sola Scriptura* folks, who claim to go by the Bible and/or who claim to model their church after the "church of the New Testament" yet don't have a ministerial priesthood that is set apart from the rest of the people with the authority, for them and no one else, to perform certain tasks involved in the worship of God—well, these folks have a problem.

And this problem is further compounded by the fact that they say the Catholic Church is unscriptural for having a ministerial or sacramental priesthood. So, not only is the Catholic Church the one following Scripture by having a sacramental priesthood, but those who are rebelling against this priesthood, saying those priests are no different than any other believer, denying that they have any special authority from God to carry out specific tasks for the people of God, just might be perishing in Korah's rebellion!

9

Makes God a Liar

How in the world, you might ask, does Protestantism make God out to be a liar? I'll tell you how. There is a part of Protestant theology called forensic justification. Forensic justification, as explained to me by Protestants, works like this: Sinful man, who is guilty of sin and deserving of Hell, appears in the courtroom over which God the Father presides as judge. Ordinarily, a sinful man would be declared guilty—since he *is* guilty—by the judge. However, if a sinful man makes an act of faith, he says the Sinner's Prayer, accepts Jesus into his heart as his personal Lord and Savior, or any such thing, then that man's sins are now covered over by the Blood of Christ. That man is now covered in the righteousness of Christ, even though he is still unrighteous.

Once sinful man's sins are covered over by the Blood of Christ, he then becomes "hid with Christ in God" (Col. 3:3). Once he is "hid with Christ," the Judge—God the Father—no longer sees a sinful man and his sins. All the Judge sees is Jesus Christ, the innocent victim Who has paid the price, with His Blood on the Cross, for all men's sins. Seeing only Jesus, He renders a verdict of innocent. This verdict of innocent is applied to all who are "hid" in Christ Jesus, all believers. The righteousness of Christ is said to be legally "imputed" to the unrighteous sinner. In this way, a believer, even though truly guilty, is "forensically," or legally, declared innocent.

In other words, all those who believe in Jesus Christ are justified or saved solely by an act of faith in Him. This is the "legal" basis for the dogma of *Sola Fide*, salvation by faith alone. A man is justified/saved at the moment he makes an act of faith. He is declared by God to be innocent of his sins at the point of having faith. That man is not actually made innocent. He is not actually sanctified or made holy. No. He is simply declared to be innocent even though he is still guilty.

After the sinner is legally declared innocent, then the process of sanctification, being made holy, begins. For the rest of his life, the sinner, through the grace of God, can grow in holiness. But from everything I've been told, he doesn't have to grow in holiness, and he is still saved. Once Saved, Always Saved.

Now, back to this thing about Protestantism making God out to be a liar. This whole business about forensic justification is why I say that. Think about it. When God says something *is,* then it *is* what He says it is! Yet in this most fundamental of Protestant dogmas, when God says it *is,* it actually *isn't.* The inward character of the sinner is not changed through the act of justification, through God's declaration. It is merely "hid."

Forensic justification puts God in the position of declaring guilty people to be innocent. But they aren't innocent. They're guilty! A person is "declared" to be in right relation to God when he really isn't in right relation to God. A person is declared to have the "status" of being just when he really isn't just. A person is declared to be *forensically* innocent when he is *actually* guilty.

There is a saying attributed to Martin Luther, although it's not certain he actually said it, that perfectly describes this concept of forensic justification. It goes something along these lines: "Sinful man, being rotten to the core, is like a pile of dung. However, once he makes a profession of faith, he becomes covered over in the righteousness of Christ, in the same way a pile of dung is covered over by a pure white fall of snow." So, the folks who are saved are, essentially, piles of dung covered over by snow. The guilty are, again, legally declared innocent by God even though they're actually still guilty.

To say something *is* when you know it really *isn't* is to lie. This whole idea of forensic justification is predicated upon God being willing to lie, God being willing to say something is when He knows it really is not. That's a lie!

Furthermore, this concept of forensic justification makes God's Word, as found in the Scriptures, a lie. Hebrews 12:14 tells us that we are to "strive for peace with all men, and for the holiness without which no one will see the Lord." The Bible, the Word of God, says that you have to be holy to see the Lord. Forensic justification says you can see the Lord whether you're holy or not; all you have to do is believe, and you are declared innocent. This means, once declared innocent (justified), you are going to see Jesus whether or not you ever become holy (sanctified). That makes a lie of Hebrews 12:14.

And that's not the only verse of Scripture that is flipped on its head if forensic justification is true. "Whoever, therefore, eats the bread or drinks the cup of the Lord in an unworthy manner will be guilty of profaning the body and blood of the Lord" (1 Cor. 11:27). Now hold on a minute, you can't be "guilty" of profaning the Body and Blood of the Lord if you're a believer, and it would only be believers who would be eating the bread or drinking the cup of the Lord, because you have been forensically declared innocent by God. God doesn't see your sins anymore because you are hid with Christ. Once you are declared innocent, you are always innocent. There is none of this "guilty" stuff for believers. I guess maybe Paul wasn't clued in on this forensic justification thing or he wouldn't have been throwing around the G word—*guilty*!

"Husbands love your wives, as Christ loved the church and gave himself up for her, that he might sanctify her, having cleansed her by the washing of water with the word, that he might present the church to himself in splendor, without spot or wrinkle or any such thing, that she might be holy and without blemish" (Eph. 5:25–27). The Church, that is the members of the Church, is cleansed by Christ in the washing of water with the Word. If the Church is cleansed, washed, without spot or wrinkle, then it is actually made innocent, not just declared innocent.

"He saved us, not because of deeds done by us in righteousness, but in virtue of his own mercy, by the washing of regeneration and renewal in the Holy Spirit" (Titus 3:5). We were saved *by* the washing of regeneration and renewal in the Holy Spirit. It doesn't say we were saved by our own declaration of belief or by being legally declared innocent even though we are guilty. It says we were saved by being washed. We were saved by being regenerated and renewed in the Holy Spirit. Whether you believe Paul to be speaking of water Baptism here, as do Catholics, or of Baptism of the Spirit, the fact is that we are saved by being washed, regenerated, and renewed. We are actually made clean. We are actually made innocent, not just legally declared so.

"Therefore, if any one is in Christ, he is a new creation; the old has passed away, behold, the new has come" (2 Cor. 5:17). This verse absolutely destroys the teaching on forensic justification. Protestant theology says you are *not* made new, that you are *not* a new creation at the moment you are "hid with Christ" and legally declared innocent. The Word of God says otherwise: a new creation, not the same old pile of dung. Forensic justification says: "No change in the man." The Word of God says: "The man has become a new creation." I'll go with the Word of God. Just a couple more verses.

"For neither circumcision counts for anything, nor uncircumcision, but a new creation" (Gal. 6:15). There's that new creation thing again. Being a new creation necessarily means that something had to change in man, at the moment of salvation, at the moment of justification.

"Truly, truly, I say to you, unless one is born anew ["born again" in the King James Version], he cannot see the kingdom of God.... Unless one is born of water and the Spirit, he cannot enter the kingdom of God" (John 3:3–5). Being "born again" means to be born of water and the Spirit. The Catholics would say this is referring to water Baptism, while the Protestant generally believes it's referring to Baptism in the Spirit. Whatever you believe, it is talking about being born "again." I don't know of a Protestant who doesn't equate that term with being saved or justified.

So, then, if forensic justification is true, that means that when one is born *again*, one is still born as a pile of dung. You're a pile of dung, then you get saved, which means you're born again as a pile of dung. Why do you have to be born again if there is absolutely no change in you? That makes no sense. Forensic justification would also mean that being born of the Spirit is, essentially, the same thing as being born of the flesh. You're born of the flesh, and you're a sinner. You're born again of the Spirit, and yep, you're still a sinner.

This idea of forensic justification makes God a liar in two ways. First, it makes God a liar, in a direct way, every time He supposedly declares a guilty person innocent even though he is not innocent. Second, it makes God a liar, in an indirect way, through all the verses of Scripture that absolutely deny the possibility of a person being able to be saved without any change in the fundamental nature of the person whatsoever. So much for a "new creation" or "regeneration" or being "washed" or having to be "holy" to see the Lord, or being without "spot" or "blemish" or "wrinkle" or anything along those lines. Nope. This pernicious doctrine says that when you're saved, you aren't regenerated, you aren't born again, you aren't washed, you sure as heck aren't holy, and you still have all those nasty spots, blemishes, and wrinkles. It says God lied.

10

Teach No Other Doctrine

This problem with Protestantism emanates from 1 Timothy 1:3: "As I urged you when I was going to Macedonia, remain at Ephesus that you may charge certain persons not to teach any different doctrine." Or as the King James Version puts it: "... that thou mightest charge some that they teach no other doctrine."

I've already tapped into the riches of this verse and the problems it presents for Protestantism in the chapter titled "There Is No Protestant Catechism (Part 1)," but I think it will serve a useful purpose to look at this verse from a different perspective.

So, why is 1 Timothy 1:3, with Paul's instruction to Timothy to make sure others "teach no other doctrine," a problem with Protestantism? Well, that's pretty obvious, isn't it? Protestantism, with its tens of thousands upon tens of thousands of denominations and non-denominations, teaches all sorts of different doctrines.

To review some of what I wrote in that chapter on there not being a Protestant catechism, you can find within Protestantism those who believe in salvation by faith alone and those who don't. You can find those who believe in the Rapture and those who don't. Among those who do believe in the Rapture, some believe in a pre-tribulation Rapture, others in a mid-tribulation Rapture, and still others in a post-tribulation Rapture. Then there are those who believe there will be more than one Rapture. You will also find those who believe in Once Saved, Always Saved and those who don't. There are those who believe in sacraments and those who don't.

You have Protestants who believe in the Trinity and those who don't. Those who have bishops and/or priests and those who don't. Those who believe in infant Baptism and those who don't. Those who believe we are born again through Baptism and those who don't. Those who believe in soul sleep and those who don't. Those who believe in the total annihilation of the damned and those who don't. Those who believe in divorce and remarriage and those who don't. Those who believe same-sex relations are moral and those who don't. Those who believe abortion is perfectly acceptable and those who don't. And I could go on and on and on.

In other words, within Protestantism, we have conflicting doctrines, conflicting moral teachings, and conflicting models of authority. Do we see that same scenario in first-century Christianity? Does the New Testament speak of anything like the doctrinal and moral confusion that we have in Protestantism and have had since the founding days of Protestantism? Does the New Testament speak of different lines of authority for different denominations? Did the deacons ordained by the apostles in Acts 6 get to vote on who would be the next pastor of Jerusalem after the apostles left town? *No* to all of the above!

This means the principles that govern Protestantism, from its beginnings down to the present day, are not the principles that governed the early Church. The free-for-all that we find in Protestantism, and have always found in Protestantism, regarding doctrine, morality, and authority did not exist in the early Church. All of this makes it very clear that Protestantism is not a valid model for Christianity. That is a problem with Protestantism.

Let's say Paul was writing to Timothy today and he gave Timothy that exact same instruction: to make sure others teach no other doctrine than what Paul taught to Timothy. What would that mean in a Protestant environment? Would Timothy have to write Paul back and say, "Dear Paul, uh, sorry to bother you, but don't you mean that I need to make sure that others not teach any different *essential* doctrine but that it's okay to teach different *nonessential* doctrine?" Can't you see Timothy writing that? Yeah, right.

If Timothy was, let's say, a Baptist minister, what would Paul's instruction mean? I'll tell you what it would mean—it would mean that the Baptist faith was the one true faith and that any faith that taught different doctrine was not the one true faith. The same could be said if Timothy was a Methodist minister, an evangelical pastor, an Anglican priest, a Church of Christ preacher, or so on. Whatever faith tradition Timothy was, Paul's exhortation in 1 Timothy 1:3 means that Timothy's faith tradition, was *the* faith tradition and that there was no other valid faith tradition. "Teach no other doctrine."

That presents a problem for Protestantism because there is no such thing as *the* one and only valid faith tradition within Protestantism. It doesn't exist! Oh, there are a few denominations—such as the Church of Christ—that actually get it and claim their faith tradition is *the* one and only correct faith tradition, but they are a very tiny minority within Protestantism to even make such a claim. The problem for them, like all of Protestantism, is that there are splits in the Church of Christ.

Now, as I mentioned in the chapter on the Protestant catechism, or lack thereof, some will say and have said that the situation within Catholicism is no different than what we find within Protestantism, that there are people within Catholicism teaching different things just like the Protestants teach different things. For example, some say no to contraception, and others say yes. Some say no to same-sex relations being moral; others say yes. Some say Jesus rose from the dead; others say He did not, and so on. But there is a big difference between the situation within Catholicism—where there is an official teaching that everyone knows and is easily discovered, while there are those who call themselves Catholic yet dissent from that official teaching—and the situation with Protestantism, where there are tens of thousands of denominations, each with its own set of official teachings, and if you dissent from them, it is perfectly acceptable to break off and form your own denomination.

Catholicism: One central authority. One set of official teachings. Dissenters from that authority or those teachings are just that, dissenters. They do not form another church within Catholicism with a separate authority structure and a separate set of official teachings.

Protestantism: Tens of thousands upon tens of thousands of central authorities. One for each denomination and non-denomination. Tens of thousands upon tens of thousands of sets of official teachings, one for each denomination and non-denomination. Dissenters from any given central authority or any given set of official teachings are not dissenters; they are merely members of a different denomination.

So, the question is: What faith tradition was Timothy a member of? Because according to Paul, you should not teach any doctrine outside of that which Paul had taught Timothy, the clear implication being Timothy's faith tradition was *the* one and only valid faith tradition. And this faith tradition of Timothy's was also, obviously, the same faith tradition as Paul's, which was given to Paul by who? Jesus Christ Himself. So, again, what faith tradition was Timothy?

There are only three possibilities:

1. Timothy was Catholic.

2. Timothy was Eastern Orthodox.

3. Timothy was one of the Protestant denominations. This would also mean that out of the tens of thousands of denominations, there is only one that could possibly be *the* faith tradition of Timothy, as given to him by Paul, as given to him by Jesus Christ.

The vast majority of Protestantism doesn't even make the claim for the existence of only one valid faith tradition, much less claim that distinction for themselves, so there is no way that Timothy was a Protestant, because 1 Timothy 1:3 makes it abundantly clear that there is indeed one, and only one, authoritative faith tradition within Christianity. Furthermore, "teach no other doctrine" completely demolishes the favorite Protestant rationalization of all the divisions within Protestantism: "We agree on the essential doctrines, even if we disagree on the nonessential doctrines." That line is exposed as being completely bogus because 1 Timothy 1:3 can in no way be interpreted as meaning "It's actually okay to teach different doctrines, as long as they're nonessential doctrines." Teach no other doctrine is a very, very big problem for Protestantism.

11

Verses Versus Verses

In my book *Blue Collar Apologetics*, I talk about four apologetics strategies that I use and teach to Catholics. The fourth of those strategies I call "But That's My Interpretation!" That strategy is built on the premise that, according to Protestant theology, every person has the right to read and interpret the Bible on his own as he feels led by the Holy Spirit. This means each and every Catholic, when discussing the meaning of this or that verse of Scripture with a Protestant, is, by the Protestant's own theology, entitled to his own interpretation of Scripture, regardless of what the Protestant claims a particular verse means.

If the Catholic says, for example, that John 6:51–58 is referring to the Real Presence of Christ in the Eucharist, and the Protestant says, "No, you're wrong, it's referring to a symbolic representation of eating Jesus' Body and drinking His Blood," then all the Catholic needs to do is reply with: "But that's *my* interpretation!"

By doing that, the Catholic has demonstrated to the Protestant that, because of the lack of an infallible teacher of Scripture in Protestant theology, the absolute best the Protestant can do in a debate about the Faith with a Catholic, or with other Protestants who have contradictory beliefs, is one person's fallible interpretation of Scripture versus the other person's fallible interpretation of Scripture. In a Protestant theological framework, there is no way to ultimately and authoritatively resolve disputes on doctrinal or moral issues between Protestant and Catholic, or even between Protestant and Protestant.

I once engaged in a series of debates with a preacher from the Campbellite Church of Christ (CoC) on several different topics, in a few different cities, over a two-to-three-year period. Every time he was introduced at one of our debates, they would mention that he had engaged in some eighty to ninety debates with ministers from various Protestant denominations.

In talking with the CoC preacher about his debates against all these other Protestants (although the CoC does not consider itself to be Protestant, it does indeed use the Protestant Bible), I realized that, for him, doctrinal matters were essentially decided by debate. One person presents the Bible verses for his belief in a particular doctrine, and the other person presents his Bible verses for his contradictory belief regarding that doctrine, and you let the people decide for themselves where the truth lies. There is no authority that can definitively decide the matter. It is, essentially, a case of my Bible verses versus your Bible verses. Verses versus verses.

But I constantly point out that it's not just a case of verses versus verses to Protestants. It is actually a case of one person's fallible interpretation of his verses versus the other person's fallible interpretation of his verses. So, it goes beyond simply verses versus verses. It is actually fallible interpretation of verses versus fallible interpretation of verses.

Which is why pretty much every time I have a dialogue, discussion, or debate with Protestants, one of the first questions I ask is: "Are you an infallible interpreter of Scripture?" Most of the time, they try to dodge this question. They don't want to answer it because they know the implication of answering that, no, they are not infallible interpreters of Scripture. The implication is they could be wrong in their interpretation.

If I'm persistent, though, some of the folks I talk to will admit that they are not infallible interpreters of Scripture. At which point I say, "So, can we agree, then, that the best you can do in this discussion, according to your own theology, is your fallible interpretation of Scripture versus my fallible interpretation of Scripture?" They hate that. Rarely will they come out and admit that is indeed the situation their theology results in: verses versus verses—fallible interpretations of verses versus fallible interpretations of verses—with no way to ultimately decide the matter. Most of the time I ask that, folks will try to dodge the question, ignore it, or switch the topic. Every now and then, I will have that question turned around on me. The fallible Protestant interpreter of Scripture will ask a question that goes something like this: "How is trusting in your fallible interpretation of the claims of the Roman Catholic Church for your salvation any better than me trusting in my fallible interpretations of the Bible for my salvation?"

That question is, actually, pretty much the best they can do in response to my question. In fact, it is the only reasonable question on this topic that Protestants have available to them. Which is why I want to spend the rest of this chapter answering that question.

What they are getting at with their question about my fallibility in interpreting the teachings of the Catholic Church is that I keep asking how any Protestant can know that what he believes is true when what he believes depends entirely on his, or someone else's, private, fallible interpretations of Scripture. Yet here I am, also a fallible human being, trusting my interpretations about the "claims of the Roman Catholic Church" with pretty much 100 percent certainty. Is that not a contradiction since we are both fallible human beings trusting in our individual interpretations for what we believe? Why can't Protestants use the same argument on me regarding my beliefs that I use on them regarding their beliefs? In other words, as the Protestant sees it, his fallible interpretations of Scripture are essentially in the same category as my fallible interpretations of the teachings of the Roman Catholic Church.

Well, not so fast. First, let it be noted that the mere fact that they have tried to turn my own question around on me by asking their question tells me that they have no response to the argument I have been making about their fallibility and what that means regarding their interpretations of Scripture, and thus their entire belief system. One person who asked me this question first tried to dismiss my argument by calling it a "red herring," but when that response was exposed as lacking any credibility or intellectual honesty whatsoever, he changed his tack and tried to use my own argument against me. After all was said and done, I pointed out that he still never attempted any legitimate response to my argument; rather, he simply ignored and deflected. So, I asked him again, "If you are not infallible in your interpretation of Scripture, then how do you have any sure way of knowing what is and is not authentic Christian doctrine and practice?" I never got an answer.

Now, regarding him or any Protestant trying to turn the question around on me, it is a fundamental error in equating what the Protestant does with what I or any Catholic does. But before I get into my direct argument for why basing one's beliefs on their own private, nonauthoritative, fallible interpretations of Scripture does not at all equate with my accepting the teachings of the Catholic Church as being authoritative and infallible, let me first build the foundation for my answer with a few statements of fact:

1. We are living in the "real" world. In other words, what the average person is able to know through their five senses is indeed reality. We are not imagining the world around us. We are not part of someone's dream. Our universe is not wholly contained in some giant's closet like the aliens in the airport locker in *Men in Black*. We are not hooked up to a giant computer that regulates our thoughts like *The Matrix*. Our world is the real world, and our senses take in information about that real world (assuming one is not on LSD or some other hallucinogenic drug).

2. Given the first statement, there are things that we can know with certainty. So, even though I am a fallible man, I can, however, state infallibly—that is, with no fear of any error—that I am married to my wife. I can state, infallibly, that I am typing these words on my computer. I can state, infallibly, that at the time of this writing, I live in Birmingham, Alabama, and I can definitely state infallibly that I love pecan pie. And there are any number of other things about myself that I can state

infallibly. So, being fallible does not mean one can never speak infallibly. Protestants quite often seem to believe otherwise, which is a fundamental flaw in their argument.

3. I can also speak infallibly on matters related to the realms of math and science, for example. I can state, infallibly, that 2 + 2 = 4. I can state, infallibly, that the derivative of $2x^3 + 9x - 7$ is $6x^2 + 9$. I can state, infallibly, that a human being needs oxygen to live. I can state, infallibly, that if you mix charcoal, saltpeter, and sulfur together, you get a crude gunpowder that, when lit, can cause a metal mailbox to burn and melt. I know all of these things from firsthand knowledge.

4. I can, however, also speak infallibly on matters of which I do not have firsthand knowledge. For example, I can state, infallibly, that the speed of light in a vacuum is approximately 186,000 miles / second. I can state, infallibly, that the primary fuel for our sun is hydrogen. I can state, infallibly, that George Washington died in 1799. I can state, infallibly, that a water molecule is two parts hydrogen and one part oxygen. I can state all these things, and more, infallibly because of the nature of the authority of those who tell me these things.

Okay, that's the foundation upon which I am going to build my answer to the Protestant question: Our world is real, and our senses help us to discern and understand reality. Since our world is real, I can infallibly state things to be true regarding matters that I know (a) about myself, (b) about math and science and other such disciplines that I know firsthand (i.e., the world around us), and (c) things about the world that I know only secondhand. I have yet to meet a Protestant who will disagree with any of those foundational points.

Now, given these four points, I will answer the Protestant's question. Yes, I am a fallible human being. I am capable of making mistakes. However, even though I am a fallible human being, I can and do speak infallibly on certain matters, as listed above. And when I say

I can speak infallibly on certain matters, just to be absolutely clear, I am simply saying that I can speak on those particular matters without fear of error. I am not saying that I am infallible in all things. So, I am a fallible human being in general yet infallible when it comes to particular subject matter.

And all of that is why I say that a Protestant deciding on doctrine and dogma for himself, based solely on his admittedly fallible interpretations of Scripture, is not the same thing as my believing the doctrine and dogma that I believe based on the authority of the Catholic Church.

Fact: There is no evidence, whatsoever, that any Protestant has the ability to infallibly interpret Scripture, that they have the ability to interpret Scripture in a way that is absolutely free from error. Every Protestant I know admits to this fact either directly or indirectly. All Protestants deny that any man can infallibly interpret Scripture.

Conclusion: Since Protestants are indeed fallible in their interpretations of Scripture, then by definition their interpretations of Scripture, which are the sole basis of their theological system, could be wrong. They could be a little wrong, or they could be a lot wrong. They could be wrong on minor points, and they could be wrong on major points. That is the necessary conclusion regarding a person's fallibility in interpreting the Scriptures. This means, necessarily, that the Protestant theological system could have errors in one or more parts of it.

Why is my methodology of belief different from the Protestant methodology of belief? Protestants are fallible human beings who have the ability, as do all human beings, to infallibly state the truth in certain areas. They have, however, admitted that they do not have that ability when it comes to interpreting Scripture. This, again, means that their theological system, built solely on their fallible interpretations of Scripture, could, and undoubtedly does, have errors in it.

Fact: My theological system, however, is not at all based on my private, non-authoritative, fallible interpretations of Scripture. In fact, my beliefs are not based on anyone's interpretation of Scripture. The Christian Faith, Christian belief, existed before a single book of the

New Testament was ever written. The Scriptures reflect the tradition of the Christian Faith, but they are not the source of the Christian Faith, as Protestants make them out to be. That is another fundamental flaw in their argument. My theological system is based on the teachings of the 2,000-year-old Catholic Church which I believe, after careful consideration of the available evidence—and there is a lot of evidence (historical, scriptural, logical)—was founded by Jesus Christ and is guided by the Holy Spirit and operates with the authority of Jesus Christ which He Himself gave to it. When I read and interpret the Bible, I do so within the parameters of the teaching as laid down by this Church founded by Jesus Christ, not within the parameters of my own imagination and understanding.

Conclusion: If the Catholic Church was indeed founded by Jesus Christ and is indeed guided by the Holy Spirit, then my theological system is indeed without error, unless someone wishes to posit that Jesus founded a church that can teach error in faith and morals and also posit that the Holy Spirit either takes occasional breaks from guiding the church or that the Holy Spirit actually guides the church into error.

Basically, it's as if we are both—Catholic and Protestant—taking a course on the Bible. The Protestant course is, essentially, a self-study course. Yes, some of them will read the Church Fathers. But they filter everything they say through the prism of their private, non-authoritative, fallible interpretations of Scripture. Yes, they read and listen to various pastors, teachers, and theologians, but they filter everything those men and women say through the prism of their private, non-authoritative, fallible interpretations of Scripture. So, again, the individual Protestant is the sole authority in his theological system. The individual Protestant is pope, pastor, and theologian in the Church of Protestantism.

The course I am taking on the Bible, however, is being taught by the author of the book. When I read Scripture, I have a guide to help me understand it, which is scriptural (see Acts 8:30–31; Neh. 8:1–8). I am not in any way, shape, or form relying on my private, non-authoritative, fallible interpretations of Scripture as the basis of my theological system. The foundation of my theological system is not built on my ability, or lack thereof, to interpret Scripture. The Protestant relies on himself. I rely on the Church.

"But," the Protestant will say, "since you are a fallible human being, John, your decisions regarding the teaching of the Catholic Church could be wrong. Your assessment of the Catholic Church as the church founded by Jesus, since you are fallible, could be wrong." This goes back to the four points I made earlier. Even though I am a fallible human being, it does not necessarily mean that every decision I make, or every conclusion I arrive at, is indeed fallible. Being fallible, in a general sense, does not preclude being infallible in a particular sense. As I demonstrated above, I can and have spoken infallibly on matters pertaining to myself, to matters of math and science that I have firsthand knowledge of, and to matters of math and science and history (and other categories as well) that I have no firsthand knowledge of.

The question becomes, though, while one can infallibly state the truth on matters pertaining to self, science, history, math, physics, and all sorts of other areas of knowledge and endeavor, can one infallibly state the truth on matters pertaining to theology? Can one infallibly state the truth in the areas of faith and morals? The Protestant answer, based on all of my past dealings with thousands of Protestants, is: "No." I find that to be an incredibly scary theology to believe in. It means God gave us no way, without any fear of error, to know for certain what is true and what is false when it comes to faith and morals. Everything, including our eternal salvation, depends solely on our ability to, hopefully, maybe, possibly get it right when it comes to interpreting Scripture. Really? That's the situation God left us with?

"Not so!" the Protestant will protest. Scripture tells us that the Holy Spirit will guide "true Christians" into all the truth. First of all, nowhere does the Bible say the Holy Spirit will guide "true Christians" into all the truth. Jesus was talking to the apostles when He said the Holy Spirit will guide "you" into all the truth (John 16:13). Second, if the Holy Spirit does indeed guide all "true Christians" into all the truth, then that means all "true Christians" should be infallible in their interpretations of Scripture. Yet Protestants claim no one is infallible in interpreting Scripture, because man's sinful nature often makes it difficult for the Holy Spirit to break through with all the truth. They want it both ways. True Christians have all the truth. True Christians don't have all the truth. The Holy Spirit guides "true Christians" into all the truth unless, of course, they are sinners, which all true Christians are. Well, in that case, the Holy Spirit can't teach them all the truth. The edifice of illogic that the Protestant theological system has built is so huge that they are unable to see it right in front of them.

However, are not the questions regarding faith and morals—the questions pertaining to our eternal salvation—way more important than questions regarding science, math, history, and so on? If God gave us the intellect to be able to infallibly know the truth on certain matters in all of these other areas, why would He not give us a way to infallibly know the truth in the most important of areas: matters pertaining to salvation, faith, and morals? Why do people believe that God gave us a book and then essentially said, "Hey guys, there's the book; each one of you can figure it out for yourselves"?

Here are the reasons why I believe the teachings of the Catholic Church to be absolutely true and without error, and why I believe the Catholic Church is our infallible guide in all things to do with faith and morals, and why these beliefs are not equivalent to a person's personal, fallible interpretations of Scripture.

1. I have studied the historical record. Through the historical record, I have come to believe that Jesus Christ was a real Person Who walked the planet around 2,000 years ago.

2. Also through that historical record, I have come to believe in the historicity, the historical accuracy, of the Scriptures.

3. Through the historical record in general and the historicity of the Scriptures in particular, and throwing in some simple logic and common sense (for example, would the apostles be

willing to suffer poverty, beatings, jail, whippings, stonings, and ultimately death for something—Jesus being God—if they knew it to be a lie?), I have come to believe that Jesus Christ is indeed God.

4. Through the Scriptures, I see that Jesus founded a church and promised the Holy Spirit to guide that church.

Is there a possibility I could be wrong on one or more of these four points? Absolutely. However, most, if not all, Protestants would agree with me on all four of these points. So, we can take those points as a given. Where Protestants will begin to disagree with me is with my next point:

5. I believe the Church founded by Jesus Christ was, and is, the Roman Catholic Church.

Why do I believe that?

(a) Because the Catholic Church claims to be the church founded by Jesus Christ 2,000 years ago in Israel. Well, just because it claims that doesn't make it so. That's true. But there are a lot of churches out there that don't even make that claim, so they can all be eliminated as possibilities for the church Jesus founded because the church Jesus founded would certainly know that it was the church Jesus founded.

(b) Because we have historical records that can trace the line of authority in the Catholic Church, and thus the existence of the Catholic Church, all the way back to Peter and the other apostles, particularly through the bishop of Rome, the pope. We have archaeological evidence that the Catholic Church dates back to the first century. No Protestant faith tradition can offer such historical or archaeological evidence. The oldest Protestant church in existence dates back, essentially, to 1517. So, we can eliminate all Protestant churches as possibilities for being the church Jesus Christ founded 2,000 years ago in Israel.

(c) Because of the physical miracles, the healings, the incorruptibles, the Eucharistic miracles, the Shroud of Turin, the tilma of Juan Diego, the raisings of the dead, and so much more that have occurred in the Catholic Church over the last 2,000 years and continue to this day.

(d) Because in the Bible, it tells us that Jesus viewed this church He founded, whichever church that is, as having authority. Authority to bind and loose on earth what would be bound and loosed in Heaven (Matt. 16:18–19; 18:18). Authority to definitively decide disputes between Christians (Matt. 18:15–17). The authority to teach all nations (Matt. 28:18–20). The authority to forgive sins (Matt. 9:6–8; John 20:21–23). The authority to teach infallibly with His authority (Luke 10:16). The authority to call councils that can infallibly declare on matters as having been declared by the Holy Spirit Himself (Acts 15:28). The authority to lay on hands (1 Tim. 4:14). The authority to command (1 Tim. 4:11). And the authority to exhort and reprove (Titus 2:15). This church is identified as the pillar and ground of the truth (1 Tim. 3:15). And this church Jesus founded and that the Holy Spirit guides must have the necessary authority to infallibly decide which books should and should not be considered the inspired, inerrant, Word of God. No Protestant church I know of even claims to have the kind of authority that we see the church of the New Testament have and that it must have if Christianity is true.

This, then, is how I will conclude: My beliefs are based not on my own authority, not on my own fallible interpretation of Scripture, not on how well I can read and understand ancient Greek and Hebrew, not on how versed I am in theology, and not on how well I am able to understand what someone writing 2,000 years ago was actually trying to say. Rather, my beliefs are based on the teaching of the Catholic Church, which I believe is the Church founded by Jesus Christ and guided by the Holy Spirit, based on the evidence of the historical records, geography, archaeology, the Church Fathers, the testimony of numerous saints and martyrs, the testimony of miracles and healings, the evidence of apostolic succession, the mere existence of this institution we call the papacy, the absolute necessity of an authoritative Church, the testimony of Scripture, and yes, the claims of the Catholic Church Herself and Her ability to back up those claims.

I will admit that all the evidence from all these different sources and disciplines that point to the Catholic Church being *the* Church founded by Jesus Christ does not prove beyond a shadow of a doubt that the Catholic Church is what She claims. If She is not what She claims, however, then I will admit the possibility that Jesus is not God. Just as I will admit the possibility that the Trinity is a lie. Just as I will admit that the Scriptures might not be inspired and might not be without error. Because if the Roman Catholic Church is not the Church founded by Jesus Christ, then the Church founded by Jesus Christ no longer exists on this earth, and I have no sure witness that Jesus is indeed God and that the Trinity is three divine Persons yet one God and that the Scriptures are the inspired and inerrant Word of God.

Here's the thing for any and every Protestant to consider: Without the Church, the Roman Catholic Church, we would know nothing of the Trinitarian God. We would not have this book we call the Bible. We would have no knowledge of this faith we call Christian. So, the belief in the inerrancy of one's own fallible interpretations of Scripture, based on no evidence other than one's own *feeling* that what one believes is indeed true, is not equivalent to my belief based on evidence from many different sources (Catholic, Protestant, Jewish, pagan, atheist) and disciplines (history, archaeology, geography, theology, philosophy) that the Roman Catholic Church is indeed the Church founded by Jesus Christ. And as such, the Catholic Church, as the pillar and ground of the truth guided by the Holy Spirit, teaches infallibly in the areas of faith and morals.

"All well and good, John," the Protestant might say, "but even if the Catholic Church was founded by Jesus and does teach infallibly, it still comes down to your fallible interpretations of the Church's teachings versus my fallible interpretations of the Bible." Actually, no, it doesn't. Remember, as I stated above, we can, as fallible human beings, actually come to know some things with certainty through the use of our senses and intellect. Also, as I stated above, the difference between the Protestant approach and the Catholic approach to the Bible is the difference between a self-study course on the Bible and a course on the Bible that is taught by the author, the Church, the Body of Christ.

The Catholic has a teacher, a guide, to understanding Scripture and to understanding the Christian Faith. The Protestant does not. We can ask questions of this teacher. This teacher can help us to understand what it is we are reading. This teacher can correct us if we come up with an errant interpretation of this or that passage or if we are confused as to what it is that is being taught. Having access to this teacher and being able to have this teacher answer our questions and provide us with feedback allows us to know, with certainty, what this teacher—the Church, the Body of Christ—is teaching us.

Think of it this way. Let's say you signed up for a course titled "The Christian Symbolism in *The Lord of the Rings*." If you're Protestant, you arrive at the class on the first day, are given a copy of *The Lord of the Rings* trilogy, and are told to read it and figure it out for yourself. If you're Catholic, you arrive at the class on the first day, are given a copy of *The Lord of the Rings* trilogy, are told to read it, and are also told that the teacher for your course will be J. R. R. Tolkien himself. Is there a difference between the two situations? Of course there is.

The Protestant can, of course, discern a good bit of the Christian symbolism in that trilogy on his own. He will be able to be absolutely certain about what some of the symbolism means. But he is going to miss some things. Plus, there will be some symbolism that he might think means this, or maybe means that, but could never be sure. There will also be some symbolism that he will get wrong. The Catholic, however, will be able to get the full spectrum of Christian symbolism found in *The Lord of the Rings* and will be able to know, with certainty, what the symbolism means because not only does he have the books but he has the author of the books teaching them.

The Catholic is, in essence, the Ethiopian eunuch in Acts 8:27–39, who acknowledged the need for a guide in order to properly understand Scripture and who, fortunately for him, had that guide right there to climb up into his chariot to explain it all to him. Philip, who was caught up in the Spirit of the Lord (Acts 8:39), was there to explain it to the Ethiopian eunuch. The Protestant is that same Ethiopian eunuch, but he does not acknowledge the need for a guide to properly understand Scripture. He thinks he can understand it just fine all on his own. And even if he does acknowledge the need for a guide, Philip is not there—no one is there—to explain the Scriptures to him. He is on his own.

It comes down to this: Protestantism—fallible interpretations of verses versus fallible interpretations of verses. Catholicism—the infallible teachings of the Church founded by Jesus Christ and guided by the Holy Spirit. Another problem with Protestantism.

12

They Don't Even Make the Claim

The Lutheran Church knows that a little over 500 years ago, Martin Luther, a Catholic priest, broke away from the Catholic Church and essentially started the Lutheran Church. Even after 500 years, the Lutheran Church knows who its founder was. And it's exceedingly likely that in another 500, or 1,000, or 1,500 years, the Lutheran Church will still know who its founder was.

The Anglican Church knows that almost 500 years ago, King Henry VIII, then the Catholic monarch of England, broke away from the Catholic Church and essentially started the Anglican Church. Even after 500 years, the Anglican Church knows who its founder was. And it's exceedingly likely that in another 500 or 1,000 or 1,500 years, the Anglican Church will still know who its founder was.

In fact, pretty much every Protestant church that I know of knows who its founder was, no matter how long ago it was founded. Wouldn't it make sense, then, that the Church founded by Jesus Christ would be out there claiming to have been founded by Jesus Christ some—oh, I don't know—2000 years ago? That makes perfect sense to me. Yet I don't know of any Protestant churches that are out there claiming to have been founded directly by Jesus Christ Himself.

Well, there is one branch of the Church of Christ that does claim to be the "original" church, but in talking to various preachers from that church (they claim not to have "pastors"), they don't really use the language of their church having been "founded" directly by Jesus.

They just more or less claim to be the "church of the New Testament" in practice. Essentially, they claim to be a restoration, if you will, of the church of the New Testament and that their practices and beliefs are the same as the church of the New Testament, but I have never heard one of them say that their church was founded directly by Jesus Christ.

They don't like the fact, when I point it out to them, that their church was, historically, founded by Thomas and Alexander Campbell back in the 1800s. They will claim that their church goes back to the first century, yet when I've asked if they can give me the name of any member of their church from the second century or fifth century or tenth century, or even the seventeenth or eighteenth centuries, or if they can give me any archaeological evidence for any of their church buildings being older than 150 years or so, things go strangely quiet.

Anyway, the point I'm making is that I am aware of no Protestant church that claims to be 2,000 years old and to have been founded directly by Jesus Christ. The Catholic Church, however, claims to have been founded directly by Jesus, through the apostles, upon the rock of Peter, 2,000 years ago. Furthermore, the Catholic Church has the historical documentation to back up those claims. Protestant churches not only have no such historical documentation, but again, they don't even make the claim!

This leads me to ask again: Wouldn't the church founded by Jesus Christ know that it was founded by Jesus Christ? And wouldn't it be out there telling folks it was founded by Jesus Christ? So, if no Protestant church or denomination even makes the claim, why should I, or anyone else for that matter, be a member of it? I want to belong to the church Jesus founded and that He sent the Holy Spirit to guide. The Catholic Church makes the claim.

In addition to that, we see that the church of the New Testament was given the authority, by Jesus, to bind and loose on earth that which will be bound and loosed in Heaven (Matt. 16:19; 18:18). Does any Protestant church have such authority? No! They don't even make the claim to have such authority. The Catholic Church makes the claim.

Speaking of this authority given by Jesus to Peter in Matthew 16:19, Jesus mentions the keys of the Kingdom of Heaven being given to Peter, and Peter alone, among the apostles. Of course, these weren't material keys; rather, the keys are spiritual in nature, keys that are the symbol of authority in this church that Jesus is starting. Well, what happened to those keys? Who has them? Does any Protestant church have the keys to the Kingdom of Heaven? No! They don't even make the claim to have them. They don't even make the claim to have the kind of authority that is represented by the keys of the Kingdom of Heaven. The Catholic Church makes the claim.

In Matthew 18:17, Jesus tells His disciples that if there is a dispute between someone and his brother, the ultimate authority for deciding that dispute is the church. He says, "If he [the brother] refuses to listen to [the witnesses], tell it to the church; and if he refuses to listen even to the church, let him be to you as a Gentile and a tax collector." In other words, if he refuses to listen to the church — the ultimate authority — then have nothing more to do with him.

Which church, though, are we supposed to "tell it to" in order to fulfill this saying of Jesus? Which church is the ultimate arbiter of disputes between Christians? Which church has the authority to rule on matters between Christians in such a way that it is binding on all Christians? Is there a Protestant church out there that fits the bill? No! They don't even claim to have the authority a church would need to be the ultimate arbiter in disputes between Christians. The Catholic Church makes the claim.

In the Bible, we see that the New Testament church called together a council—the Council of Jerusalem (Acts 15)—to decide a doctrinal dispute that was ongoing between some of the Jewish Christians and the Gentile Christians. The church of the Council of Jerusalem came to a decision that was then seen as binding on all Christians. I don't know how many times I've heard various Protestant churches claiming (the Church of Christ being a perfect example) to be doing things the way the Christians in the Bible did things. Yet when it comes to doctrinal disputes among Christians, is there a Protestant church out there that has called a council and come to a doctrinal decision to which they claim the authority to hold all Christians everywhere as being bound by that decision? No! They don't even make the claim to have the authority to call together such a council. The Catholic Church makes the claim.

What else do we see from the Bible as being characteristic of the Church Jesus founded? Well, what was the nature of all of this authority I've been talking about? It was the authority of Jesus Christ Himself as given to the apostles (John 20:21–23; Matt. 28:18–19). So, we could say it is apostolic authority: authority that was passed on through the laying on of hands as we see, for example, in Paul's letters to Timothy. It is apostolic authority that, if Jesus' Church is still in existence, should have been passed down to the leaders of the Church today. Does apostolic authority exist in any Protestant churches today? No! They don't even make the claim. The Catholic Church makes the claim.

We see also that the leaders of this Church claimed to speak for the Holy Spirit (Acts 15:28). If they did indeed speak on behalf of the Holy Spirit, it means they spoke infallibly on the doctrinal matters they were deciding. Does any Protestant church speak infallibly on behalf of the Holy Spirit in deciding doctrinal disputes? No! They don't even make the claim. The Catholic Church makes the claim.

To summarize all of this, the Bible describes for us some of the elements that characterize this church Jesus founded: the authority to bind and loose, the authority to call councils, the authority to decide disputes, the authority to speak on behalf of the Holy Spirit, and so on. Authority, authority, authority! Authority that was apostolic in nature. We also know that this church Jesus founded, if it still exists, has to be 2,000 years old.

The Catholic Church claims all of these things for herself, and more. She claims to be able to speak infallibly on doctrinal matters. She claims to be able to trace the line of her authority back to the apostles and, through the apostles, to Jesus Christ. She claims to have been founded directly by Jesus Christ and to be 2,000 years old. Does the fact that the Catholic Church makes all of these claims prove that these claims are true? No. But upon closer examination, she can indeed back up all of the claims she makes.

The Protestant churches and denominations? They don't even make the claim.

PART 2

Questions Protestants Can't Answer

Question 1

Is a Dead Body Really a Body?

Now, you might be thinking, "*What?*" What does that question have to do with the Bible or with Protestant theology? Well, actually, it has a lot to do with the Bible and Protestant theology. The vast majority of Protestants believe in this dogma known as *Sola Fide*, which means "salvation by faith alone," where we are saved by our faith — alone — and works have nothing at all to do with our salvation.

Yet when I point out to them many of the Scripture passages that show the necessity of works in relation to salvation—for example, Matthew 25:31–46, Romans 2:6–7, and James 2:14–17 (as well as many others)—what I am told is that we are indeed saved by faith alone, but if we have *true* faith, it will be accompanied by good works. As I have heard more than one Protestant put it, "We are saved by faith alone, but true faith is never alone," which I believe is a quote, or a paraphrase of a quote, from Martin Luther. They'll go on to assert that faith without works really isn't faith. So, yes, works are definitely important, they'll say, but again, they have absolutely nothing to do with our salvation.

According to this line of reasoning, which Protestant theology has developed to get around all of the Bible passages that speak of works being related to salvation, even if someone *says* he has faith, if his faith isn't accompanied by works, then he doesn't really have faith. Faith without works isn't *really* faith. The problem for those who make this argument, however, is that the Bible nowhere says such a thing. James

2:17 says, "So faith by itself, if it has no works, is dead." It doesn't say, "So faith by itself, if it has no works, isn't really faith."

After I point out James 2:17 to them, that's when I ask: "Is a dead body really a body?" The first response I usually get is, "What?" So, I'll say again, "Is a dead body really a body; yes or no? Are all the bodies down at the morgue real bodies?" Every time I ask, the answer is always, "Yes, a dead body is really a body." "Well," I say, "if a dead body is really a body, then a dead faith is really faith." I get objections about how you can't compare a dead body to dead faith and other such arguments, which is when I take them to James 2:26, which absolutely destroys the Protestant argument that dead faith isn't really faith.

"For as the body apart from the spirit is dead, so faith apart from works is dead" (James 2:26). The Word of God is making an analogy here between the body and the spirit on the one hand, and faith and works on the other. The body is, according to James, analogous to faith, and the spirit is analogous to works. Just as the body and spirit are both necessary for life, then, for the analogy to hold, faith and works are both necessary for life. Physical life requires body and spirit; spiritual life requires faith and works.

Nowhere does the analogy say, nor even imply, that a body without a spirit really isn't a body. It is indeed a real body. It's just a real *dead* body. Just so, for the analogy to hold, faith without works is indeed a real faith. It's just a real *dead* faith, as James 2:17 confirms.

This means Protestant theology is in a bit of a bind here. If faith without works really is faith, then that means one cannot be saved by faith alone because faith, by itself, according to the Word of God, is dead. And no one is going to argue that you can be saved by a dead faith alone. James 2 absolutely destroys the dogma of salvation by faith alone. James shows us that faith alone, by definition, is dead. Faith alone — faith without works — is like the body without the soul ... dead. *Sola corpus* = dead body. *Sola Fide* = dead faith. And dead faith cannot save anyone.

That's why the question, "Is a dead body really a body?" is a question that Protestants can't answer. They can't answer it because if they say, "Yes, a dead body really is a body," then, because of the analogy in James 2:26, they have to admit that a dead faith—a faith without works—really is faith. This means one of the central tenets of Protestantism, salvation by faith alone (*Sola Fide*), is a bankrupt dogma because dead faith cannot save.

But if they try to answer the question by saying that a dead body really isn't a body, then they show themselves to be intellectually dishonest and willing to say anything, no matter how ridiculous, to try and salvage their broken theology.

Question 2

If a Man Has Faith but Has Not Works, Can His Faith Save Him?

This is a question straight out of the Bible. "What does it profit, my brethren, if a man says he has faith but has not works? Can his faith save him?" (James 2:14). It's a simple yes or no question. So, why is this a question Protestants can't answer? Because if they answer, "Yes, his faith can save him," then they run into an immediate problem with James 2:15–17: "If a brother or sister is ill-clad and in lack of daily food, and one of you says to them, 'Go in peace, be warmed and filled,' without giving them the things needed for the body, what does it profit? So faith by itself, if it has no works, is dead."

In other words, a "Yes" answer runs directly counter to the answer given by Scripture itself. But if they answer "No" to the question, then they don't really believe in salvation by faith alone, do they? By answering "No," the Protestant is essentially admitting that works are a necessary part of the process of salvation. So either way—*yes* or *no*—the Protestant has a problem to overcome. If they answer one way, it runs contrary to Scripture. If they answer the other way, it runs contrary to their theology.

Now, one way someone might try to get around this is by saying, "John, you left out a crucial part of the verse in your question. Verse 14 doesn't say, 'If a man has faith but has not works'; it says, 'If a man *says* he has faith but has not works.' What this verse is *really* talking about is when a man 'says' he has faith but he doesn't really have it.

He thinks he has faith, but he really doesn't. So, it's because of his lack of faith that he can't be saved. That's why James asked the question: 'Can his faith save him?'"

Two things here: (1) Whenever someone says to you, "What this verse means is ..." or the even more emphatic, "What this verse *really* means is ..." you immediately know that they are about to give you their private, non-authoritative, fallible interpretation of Scripture. To which you are always free to reply, "I believe what that verse says; however, I don't necessarily agree with your fallible interpretation of that verse." And if their fallible interpretation of that verse runs contrary to the teaching of the Catholic Church — which it will most of the time — then you definitely do not agree with it.

(2) There is a problem with their interpretation in that the question James asks is, "Can his faith save him?" James didn't ask, "Can his so-called faith save him?" Or, "Can his supposed faith save him?" Or, "Can his lack of faith save him?" Or anything else along those lines. Why ask if a man's faith can save him if the man has no faith? That makes no sense. It especially makes no sense in light of verse 17. Does verse 17 read, "So faith by itself, if it has no works, really isn't faith"? No! That would be like saying, "So a body, by itself, if it has no soul, really isn't a body." (Where have I heard that before?) Verse 17 says, "So faith by itself, if it has no works, is dead." And, as I showed in Question #1, dead faith is really faith. It's just dead. It does not bring life.

Furthermore, James 2 goes on to say that "faith apart from works" — that is, faith alone — "is barren" (v. 20). It also states that faith is "completed by works" (v. 22). Then, verse 24, "You see that a man is justified by works and not by faith alone." Faith and works are both necessary components of the process of salvation — both being accomplished by the grace of God.

Thus, we have another question Protestants can't answer.

Question 3

Can Someone through Well-Doing (i.e., Good Works) Receive Eternal Life?

For the Protestant who believes in *Sola Fide*—salvation by faith alone—the obvious and immediate answer to this question is a re-sounding "No!" But once again, we see that the Protestant answer runs directly contrary to what Scripture says. In Romans 2:6–7, we see the Word of God tell us the following: "For he will render to every man according to his works: to those who by patience in well-doing seek for glory and honor and immortality, he will give eternal life."

So, a "No" answer from the Protestant leads to a conflict with Scripture, but a "Yes" answer from the Protestant once again runs contrary to their *Sola Fide* theology. Of course, I have had a number of folks try to explain this passage to me in such a way that they can get around the very plain meaning of the words. They usually say something along the lines of, "John, what this passage means is that those who do good works will be rewarded *in* Heaven for those good works. It doesn't mean they will be rewarded *with* Heaven for those good works. They'll just be given a higher place in Heaven." Ohhh … I see. Actually, no, I don't see.

There's just one problem with that explanation, well, a couple of problems. First, Romans says, straight up, that those who patiently do these good works while seeking for glory and honor and immortality will be given, by God, *eternal life*! It doesn't say they will be rewarded with a higher place *in* Heaven for those good works. It says they will be rewarded *with* Heaven.

This is one of those times where you ask anyone who says otherwise, "Where does the passage say what you say it says?" The Protestant says the verse is talking about a reward *in* Heaven and not *of* Heaven. Where does the Bible say that? It doesn't. Once again, the Protestant is trying to force his fallible interpretation into the Bible. He is trying to fit the Bible to his beliefs rather than the other way around.

The second problem with what they're saying here is found in verses 8–10: "But for those who are factious and do not obey the truth, but obey wickedness, there will be wrath and fury. There will be tribulation and distress for every human being who does evil, the Jew first and also the Greek, but glory and honor and peace for every one who does good, the Jew first and also the Greek." The contrast between verses 7 and 8 and then between verses 9 and 10 is a contrast between salvation and damnation, a contrast between eternal life and wrath and fury.

If verse 7 is simply referring to those who do good being rewarded with a higher place in Heaven, then verse 8 should be referring to those who don't do good as being given a lower place in Heaven. However, there is no wrath and fury nor tribulation and distress in Heaven. Verses 8 and 9 are clearly referring to eternal damnation. So, what we have here in all of these verses is eternal salvation being juxtaposed with eternal damnation. Heaven or Hell. Those who do good and those who do evil. We do not have the handing out of higher or lower places in Heaven.

Now, as Catholics, we do not take this to mean that it is our works alone that save us. We take Scripture in its entirety. We don't allow one verse of Scripture to "trump" another verse of Scripture. But this passage from Romans 2 very clearly shows the importance of good works in the process of salvation. Again, as I have said elsewhere, a passage like this in no way implies salvation by works alone (as always, any passage has to be read in the larger context of all of Scripture), but it definitely rules out salvation by faith alone.

This is a question that Protestants can't answer. At least, not in a scripturally consistent, theologically consistent, and/or logically consistent manner.

Question 4

Who Wrote the Gospel of Mark?
How Do You Know?

This question goes to the very heart of *Sola Scriptura*. If there is one dogma that is nearly universal among Protestants, it is the dogma of *Sola Scriptura*, the belief that we, as Christians, can find out all we need to know about the Christian Faith and Christian morality by simply picking up the Bible and reading it. It is the Bible, and the Bible alone, we Christians are to go by as our sole authority in matters of faith and morals. Although there are some Protestants who say that the Bible is not our *sole* authority as Christians, it is indeed their sole *infallible* authority. Either way, it doesn't really matter regarding this question.

What does matter, though, is the fact that nowhere in the Bible does it tell you who wrote the Gospel of Mark. Was it actually someone named Mark? Or is that just a pseudonym? Was this Mark a disciple of Jesus? Or was he just some Joe Shmoe who read Matthew or Luke and decided he was going to write something about this Jesus guy too? Nowhere does the Bible tell us. Although, I did have someone say to me once, "The Bible does tell you that Mark wrote the Gospel of Mark. It's right there in the table of contents. It says, 'The Gospel of Mark.'" Um, no. The table of contents is not inspired Scripture. It is put in the Bible by the publisher.

Regardless, the vast majority of Protestants believe, as do Catholics, that the writer of the Gospel of Mark is the Saint Mark who was the companion and disciple of both Peter and Paul. But the question is:

How do we know that? How does any Protestant know that? If I go by the Bible alone regarding all matters pertaining to the Christian Faith yet nowhere does the Bible tell me that Mark, the disciple of both Peter and Paul, wrote the Gospel of Mark, then it seems to me I have a little bit of a problem.

The problem is that I have to go to some authority outside of the Bible in order to find out who wrote the Gospel of Mark. And not just who wrote the Gospel of Mark, but if the author of that Gospel was indeed inspired by the Holy Spirit so that we may have certainty when we read it that we are not just reading the word of man but are indeed reading the Word of God. But if I am relying on some authority outside of the Bible to tell me that one or more of the books of the Bible are the inspired Word of God, then doesn't that fly in the face of the dogma of *Sola Scriptura*?

Think about it. In order to know that the Gospel of Mark is the inspired, inerrant Word of God and that it was indeed written by Saint Mark, I have to rely on some authority outside of the Bible to tell me this very critical piece of information about the Bible and about the very foundation of my Christian Faith. Now, as I mentioned, there are those Protestants who will say that they're okay with having to rely on an authority outside of the Bible. They're okay with the Bible not being the *sole* authority for Christians. But they insist that it is the sole *infallible* authority for Christians.

Oh, really? Well, if that's the case, then we have another problem or two for this line of thinking. The first problem is that we still haven't answered the question: How do you know? Who, or what, is this authority outside of the Bible that we are relying on in order to be sure that the Gospel of Mark, or really any other book of the Bible, is the inspired, inerrant Word of God? What authority are we relying on?

I debated a Church of Christ preacher one time on the topic of *Sola Scriptura*, and I asked him this same question. His answer? "We know that the Gospel of Mark is the inspired, inerrant Word of God because of the witness of the early Christians!" I about fell out of my chair. When it was my turn at the podium, I turned to the preacher and said, "Do you know what Catholics call the 'witness of the early Christians'? Tradition!" That preacher does not believe in Tradition as a source of authoritative teaching. In fact, "Tradition" is something along the lines of a cussword for many Protestants.

But still, he didn't say which early Christians, when they lived, where they lived, or what authority they had to declare Mark was indeed the inspired, inerrant Word of God. He dared not say it was the Christians, and the bishops in particular, of the Catholic Church, whose witness and authority we rely on to know that the Gospel of Mark is indeed the Word of God.

Finally, there is one last problem for the Protestants here: If the Bible is the *only* infallible authority for Christians, then that means this extra-biblical authority we've been talking about, the one that vouched for the various books of the Bible as being inspired Scripture, is not infallible. This means they could have made a mistake or two when putting the Bible together or when they were deciding which books were or were not the inspired Word of God. That's what being fallible means—you can make mistakes.

So, in the end, Protestants can, at best, have a fallible list of supposedly infallible books, but they can't know for sure. That's why this is a question Protestants can't answer because they have to rely on some fallible authority *outside* of the Bible in order to have their Bible in the first place. Relying on this extra-biblical authority completely puts the lie to the dogma of *Sola Scriptura*. It can't be true if you have to rely on an authority outside of Scripture in order to have Scripture in the first place.

Question 5

Is Faith Greater than Love?

Saint Paul, in 1 Corinthians 13:13, says this: "So faith, hope, love abide, these three; but the greatest of these is love." I have heard or read this verse many times over the years. But on one occasion of reading this verse, it occurred to me that, were I a believer in *Sola Fide*, salvation by faith alone, then this verse would, if I really thought about it, cause me a bit of a problem.

Here's the thing: If salvation—spending eternity in Heaven with the Father, Son, and Holy Spirit—is the absolute greatest thing that could ever happen to us, which it is, and faith alone is the means by which we are granted salvation, which it is (according to *Sola Fide*), then why is love greater than faith? That doesn't make any sense to me. Faith should be greater than love if *Sola Fide* is true.

So even though the scriptural answer to the question above is, "No, faith is not greater than love," it seems that from a *Sola Fide* perspective, which tells us that faith is what gets us to Heaven for all of eternity, the answer ought to be, "Yes, faith *is* greater than love."

What could be greater than that one thing, and that one thing only, that gains for the individual believer the greatest gift possible: salvation? What could be greater? Love? *Really?* Love is a wonderful and awesome thing. However, according to *Sola Fide*, love does absolutely nothing for us in terms of our salvation. Yet that's what the Bible tells us: that love is greater than faith.

If a Protestant answers this question with a "No" and says that faith is not greater than love, then he needs to explain why that is since love has nothing to do with our salvation and faith has everything to do with our salvation (according to his theology). If, however, he answers that faith is indeed greater than love, then he is clearly at odds with the Word of God in 1 Corinthians 13:13.

Thus, a question Protestants can't answer.

Question 6

Was the Prodigal Son Saved before
He Left His Father's House?

Everyone knows the Parable of the Prodigal Son from chapter 15 of the Gospel of Luke. A man had two sons, and one day the younger son came to his father and asked for his share of the inheritance. Essentially, the younger son was saying to his father, "You are dead to me. Give me, now, what I would otherwise inherit from you upon your death." So, the father gives him the share of the property that was his inheritance, and the son goes off to a foreign land. In this foreign land, the prodigal son engaged in a sinful lifestyle and wound up squandering everything his father had given him. He was broke and starving.

At this low point in his life, the prodigal son realizes that he has been a fool, and he repents of his sinful living and decides to go back to his father and ask for forgiveness. As he is on his way back to his father's house, his father sees him coming from a distance and runs to greet him. After greeting his son, the father declares a feast and says, "For this my son was dead, and is alive again; he was lost, and is found" (Luke 15:24).

The key word in that verse is *again*. The son is alive *again*! Which would mean that the son was alive, then he was dead, and then he was alive again. Think about how this verse relates to the Protestant dogma of Once Saved, Always Saved, which is the belief that once a person is saved—once he has said the Sinner's Prayer or accepted Jesus Christ into his heart as his personal Lord and Savior—then he cannot lose his salvation. He cannot become unsaved. His ticket for the train to Heaven has been punched, and there is nothing that can derail that train. Once he is saved, he is always saved.

Luke 15:24, however, seems to fly in the face of Once Saved, Always Saved. The parable starts off with the younger son living in his father's house. He is in good standing with his father. He is *alive* to his father. But then the son takes his inheritance and goes off to live a life of sin, at which point he is *dead* to the father (and the father is dead to him). Then the son repents of his sins and seeks forgiveness from the father, at which point the son is said to be alive *again*.

The father in this parable has always been seen, by Christians of all stripes — Catholic and non-Catholic alike — as representing God the Father. Just so, the prodigal son represents sinful humanity. When we repent of our sins and turn to God for forgiveness, our loving Father will indeed forgive us.

Now, looking at this parable through the lens of salvation, what do we see? The son is in good standing with his father. He is living in his father's house. He is alive to the father. In salvation terms, being "alive" is, essentially, the same as being "saved." "But if Christ is in you ... your spirits are *alive*" (Rom. 8:10). But then the son rejects his father and goes and lives a sinful life and squanders his inheritance. He is described, by his father, as having been "dead" while living in sin. Being dead, in salvation terms, is the same as being unsaved. We see in Revelation 20:14–15 that eternal damnation is referred to as the second *death*. Physical death is the first death; spiritual death is the second death. So, again, being dead in a salvation sense is the same as being unsaved.

Given all of that, the Parable of the Prodigal Son absolutely puts a dagger into the heart of the Once Saved, Always Saved dogma. The son starts out being alive (saved), then he sins, which causes him to be dead to the father (unsaved), and then in the end, he repents, asks for forgiveness, and is alive (saved) again. If Once Saved, Always Saved is true, then Luke 15:24, instead of saying, "For this my son was dead, and is alive again," should have said, "For this my son was alive, and is still alive."

Let's go back to the original question and why Protestants can't answer it. It is very obvious from the parable that the prodigal son was "alive" and in his father's house before he demanded his share of the inheritance and went off to live a sinful life. But if the Once Saved, Always Saved Protestant says he was indeed alive, or saved, before he left his father's house, then he has basically contradicted his own theology because that means the son was saved, lost his salvation by sinning, then was saved *again*.

But if he denies that the son was originally in a state of being saved before he left his father's house, then he needs to come up with a really good explanation for how that can be, especially since the son received his inheritance from the father. What is the "inheritance" of a son of God? Of a Christian? Heaven. Eternal life. "So that those who are called may receive the promised eternal inheritance" (Heb. 9:15).

The Parable of the Prodigal Son doesn't just show us that we have a loving and merciful Father in Heaven Who will forgive us if we come to Him in humility and ask for that forgiveness. It also highlights the fact that we can lose our inheritance, eternal life, by sinning against the Father. We can go from being alive in Christ to being dead in our sins.

Once Saved, Always Saved? I don't think so.

Question 7

Are You an Infallible Interpreter of Scripture?

Most of these questions Protestants can't answer emanate from a particular verse, or passage, of Scripture. This question, however, is more of a general biblical question. I am often told, as a Catholic, that my beliefs or my interpretations of Scripture are not correct, that my beliefs are not found in Scripture, or that my beliefs actually contradict Scripture. So, I ask people who say such things to me: "Are you an infallible interpreter of Scripture? Are your interpretations of the Bible infallible? Yes or no?"

I ask that because the basis for someone telling me that I'm wrong—that my interpretations of the Bible are wrong, that my Catholic beliefs are wrong—is nothing more than their personal interpretation of Scripture. They are not basing their claims on some church's authority or on some pastor's authority. They're basing their claims on how they, as individuals, read and interpret the Bible.

Thus the question: "Are you an infallible interpreter of Scripture?" Pretty much every Protestant will say that not only is the pope not infallible but that no man is infallible. Well, if no man is infallible, then that means when a Protestant interprets Scripture, which they do every time they read Scripture or talk to a Catholic about Scripture, and they try to tell me that I'm wrong and that my beliefs are not biblical—based on their interpretations of Scripture—they could be wrong! The private interpretations of any and every Protestant are fallible, so there is at least the *possibility* they could be wrong.

Most Protestants have never considered the fact that since they are not infallible, and therefore capable of making mistakes, then that means their interpretations of Scripture are, necessarily, *fallible* interpretations. Their interpretations of Scripture could, quite possibly, be wrong. That thought never enters their mind. This means that every time—every single time—you as a Catholic are told that your beliefs are wrong, that the Catholic Church teaches heresy, that Catholic teaching on this or that doctrine is contrary to the Bible, that you are not interpreting the Bible properly, and so on, then the person saying those things to you, not being an infallible interpreter of Scripture, has to admit that everything he is saying to you could possibly be wrong.

This gives each and every Catholic, each and every time he gets into a discussion or dialogue with a Protestant who quotes some Bible verse to "prove" Catholic teaching is wrong, the right to say: "I, as a Catholic, believe that verse. In fact, as a Catholic, I believe every single verse of the Bible. However, I do not agree with your fallible interpretation of that verse." Or if the Catholic quotes a verse of the Bible as evidence in support of some Catholic doctrine, and he is told, "That's not a correct interpretation of Scripture," he can simply ask: "Are you an infallible interpreter of Scripture? If not, can you infallibly tell me that I'm wrong?"

What will quite often happen, when you start pointing out that the private interpretations of Scripture done by fallible persons are necessarily fallible interpretations of Scripture, is that the Protestant will try to either deflect your question or simply ignore it altogether. He may try to deflect by saying, "Well, that means that your interpretations of Scripture are also not infallible interpretations." To which I immediately agree. "Yes, my private interpretations of Scripture are not infallible." I then add, "Which means, that in our discussion here, the best you can do, according to your theology, is your fallible interpretation of Scripture versus my fallible interpretation of Scripture."

Think about that. As a Catholic, any time you engage in a discussion on matters of faith and the Bible and the Church and such with a Protestant, the best the Protestant can do is give you his fallible interpretations of Scripture versus your fallible interpretations of Scripture. I don't care if you're talking to some theologian with five PhDs in Scripture study; it's still his fallible interpretation of Scripture versus your fallible interpretation of Scripture. Under his theology, that is the best he can do, whether he is talking to a Catholic or to a fellow Protestant who has different beliefs than he does. The problem is: Who has the authority to definitively say this view is right and this other view is wrong? Who has the authority to definitively decide disputes between Christians on matters of faith? In Protestantism, the answer is no one.

Now, I once had the pastor of a so-called Bible church, after I had explained to him the meaning of a particular verse of Scripture in relation to some Catholic doctrine, say to me, "Just a minute, John! You just said a few minutes ago that the best you can do is your fallible interpretation of Scripture versus my fallible interpretation of Scripture." To which I replied, "No, pastor, I said that's the best you can do, given your theology. The best I can do, given my theology, is the infallible teaching of the Church founded by Jesus Christ and guided by the Holy Spirit versus your fallible interpretations of Scripture." Well, needless to say, he didn't like that very much. It kind of stunned him. He had never been faced with an argument like that. But it's true. I do not rely on my fallible interpretations of Scripture as the basis for what I believe and teach. I rely on the infallible teaching of the Church Jesus founded. And as long as my fallible interpretations of Scripture do not stray outside the bounds of Church teaching, then I am on solid ground.

So, this is a question Protestants can't answer because if they answer in accordance with their theology, then they have to say that, no, they are not infallible interpreters of Scripture. But that then opens the door for you to inform them that everything they believe about the Christian Faith, since it is based on private, fallible interpretations of Scripture, could be wrong. That's a very scary thought if you take a moment to truly ponder it. Do you want to bet the eternal destination of your soul on something that could *possibly* be wrong? Furthermore, everything they believe about the Catholic Faith, since it is also based on private, fallible interpretations of Scripture, could be wrong.

One last point to note on this question is something I call being "fallible in theory, infallible in practice." If, when talking to a Protestant, any Protestant, you lead with this question: "Is any man infallible?" he will reply 100 percent of the time: "No, no man is infallible." But when you then ask him if he is an infallible interpreter of Scripture, it will be the rare Protestant who comes right out and admits that he is not. He will try to talk all around the question. Why is that? Because once you ask that question, the person you're asking will almost immediately recognize the implications of your question. The implications being that there is a chance—maybe small, maybe large—that at least something, if not everything, he says to you about the Bible and the Catholic Faith could be wrong. He is, in essence, asking you to gamble the destination of your immortal soul on his fallible interpretations of the Bible. Sorry, but no thanks.

What Protestants will often do, again, is hem and haw, deflect your question, or ignore it altogether. But here's the thing. They will continue to talk to you as if everything they are saying about their Bible interpretations and Catholic teaching and your scriptural interpretations is indeed infallible. They never say anything along the lines of, "Well, if my interpretation of this verse is correct," or, "In my opinion this verse means," or anything else along those lines. No, they speak boldly and emphatically, and they know beyond a shadow of a doubt that they are right and the Catholic is wrong. They do not even consider the possibility that they could be wrong or that the Catholic could be right. That's why I call it being fallible in theory, infallible in practice.

That attitude, though, should in no way discourage you from asking, over and over if necessary, "Are you an infallible interpreter of Scripture?" Just be aware of the attitude and be prepared to deal with it.

Question 8

Was the Flesh That Jesus Gave for the Life of the World Real or Symbolic?

This question that Protestants can't answer centers on John 6:51. Whenever there is a discussion about John 6 and whether Jesus is speaking in a literal sense about eating His flesh and drinking His blood (as Catholics believe) or whether He is speaking in a symbolic sense (as the vast majority of Protestants believe), the focus is generally on verses 52–58. John 6:51 quite often gets ignored. That shouldn't happen, though, because John 6:51 is the key to properly understanding John 6:52–58.

John 6:51 states: "I am the living bread which came down from heaven; if anyone eats of this bread, he will live for ever; and the bread which I shall give for the life of the world is my flesh." Jesus is saying that the bread that He will give us to eat is His flesh which He will give for the life of the world. So the question I always ask after reading John 6:51 to someone is this: "When did Jesus give His flesh for the life of the world?" The answer I get back 100 percent of the time, without any hesitation, is: "On the Cross." Jesus gave His flesh for the life of the world on the Cross. Right answer.

Every Christian knows that's the right answer. That's when I follow up with: "Was the flesh on the Cross, the flesh Jesus gave for the life of the world, real or symbolic?" At first glance, this question is easy to answer, right? I mean, what Christian worth his salt would ever say it was only Jesus' symbolic flesh on the Cross and not His real flesh? Some heretics did say, in the early centuries of the Church, that it wasn't really human flesh on the Cross, that Jesus looked like He had a real human body but that it was actually some type of illusion. Maybe it was more along the lines of what we might call a hologram today. It seemed real but wasn't. But I don't know any Christians who say such a thing today. Some will say, as do the Muslims, that it only "seemed" like He died on the Cross, but they don't ever say it wasn't really Him, with His real human flesh, on the Cross.

So, the first instinct of every Christian is to say that, of course, the flesh on the Cross was indeed real. The blood shed on the Cross was indeed real. And most do immediately answer by saying, "It was real flesh." However, there are a few who hesitated when I asked them this question. Why did they hesitate? Because after you've read John 6:51 to them, they realize the very obvious implication of answering, "It was real flesh," instead of, "It was symbolic flesh." The obvious implication is that John 6:51, when you follow it through, is actually saying this: "I am the living bread which came down from heaven; if anyone eats of this bread, *which is my real flesh that I will give on the cross for the life of the world,* he will live forever."

Boom! John 6:51 tends to blow a pretty big hole in Protestant theology that teaches Jesus is talking symbolically about eating His flesh and drinking His blood. The quote from John 6:51 that I have above is from the Revised Standard Version Catholic Edition of the Bible. The way the King James Version, a Protestant Bible, reads John 6:51, though, makes an even stronger case for the "real" interpretation. "I am the living bread which came down from heaven: if any man eat of this bread, he shall live for ever: and the bread that I will give is my flesh, which I will give for the life of the world" (John 6:51 KJV). "If any man eat of this bread ..." What bread? "The bread that I will give is my flesh." Your real flesh or Your symbolic flesh? The flesh "which I will give for the life of the world." Which, everyone has already agreed, was His real flesh.

So, if you say His death on the Cross was real, His flesh on the Cross was real, His blood spilled on the Cross was real, then what you're saying is that the bread He wants to give us to eat in John 6:51 is the real flesh that He gave for the life of the world on the Cross. You can't say, on the one hand, that the bread Jesus wants to give us is His *symbolic* flesh and then turn around and say, yes, the flesh He gave for the life of the world was His real flesh. You can't have it both ways. The bread is either real flesh or symbolic flesh. It can't be both.

Now, I've had a few argue, "Well, yes, the bread He's talking about is His real flesh that He gave on the Cross, but He's talking about us symbolically eating His real flesh here in John 6:51." Sorry, but no. That verse says nothing about symbolically eating anything. It talks about actually eating this bread that Jesus wants to give us. So, again, the question is: "Is the bread He wants to give us to eat real or symbolic?" To answer that, we look at the rest of the verse. Jesus says He is the living bread that came down from Heaven. Was Jesus real or symbolic? Real. Jesus says this bread He wants us to eat is His flesh which He will give for the life of the world. Was His flesh on the Cross real or symbolic? Real.

So, it is very clear that Jesus wants to give us His real flesh—the flesh that was nailed to the Cross for the life of the world—to eat so that we may live forever. And He repeats this another five or six times in the following verses. The Protestant reading of this passage would have you believe that Jesus was talking about His real flesh as the living bread to start off in John 6:51, then switched to talking about eating His symbolic flesh, then switched back to giving His real flesh for the life of the world (all in John 6:51), and then switched back again to talking about eating His symbolic flesh in verses 52–58. Yeah, right.

Sorry, but if the bread in John 6:51 that Jesus gives for the life of the world is the real flesh that He gave on the Cross, then John 6:52–58 is talking about giving us His real flesh to eat and His real blood to drink. John 6:51 is the key for the following verses. If the flesh on the Cross was real, then John 6:51 and following is talking about eating His real flesh and drinking His real blood. Only if the flesh on the Cross was symbolic, which would mean He wants us to eat His symbolic flesh that He gave for the life of the world, can you say that Jesus is talking symbolically in verses 52–58. It has to be one or the other, all the way through.

So, this is a question Protestants can't answer, because if they do indeed answer it correctly by saying Jesus gave His real flesh for the life of the world, then they have thrown a scriptural wrench into the rest of their theology, which says Jesus was only speaking symbolically in John 6:52–58. And they would need to take a good long, thoughtful, and prayerful look at Catholic teaching on the Eucharist.

Question 9

Where in the Bible Is the List or Chart of Essential versus Nonessential Doctrines?

This question was born out of the many, many times I have heard a Protestant tell me why they attack various parts of Catholic teaching — Mary, Purgatory, Sacred Tradition, the sacraments, and so on — yet rarely, if ever, question or attack the teachings of the various Protestant denominations who also have doctrines that they disagree with. For instance, you might have a Baptist talking about a Methodist or an evangelical talking about a Presbyterian, and they'll say something along the lines of, "You know, we might disagree on the nonessential doctrines, but we agree on the essential doctrines."

Well, I got to thinking as to just who it is that decides what is an essential doctrine and what is a nonessential doctrine. For example, a lot of Protestant denominations will tell you infant Baptism isn't an essential doctrine since they believe Baptism is merely a symbolic act done by the already saved believer. So, they'll say, "Since it's a 'nonessential' doctrine, it's okay to disagree on it since nonessential doctrines don't affect your salvation."

Again, most Protestants don't believe in infant Baptism, or in Baptism in general, as being more than just a symbolic act. However, there are the Lutherans and the Episcopalians, and possibly others, who believe that Baptism is how we are born again, that we are regenerated through Baptism, and that it is through Baptism we become members of the Body of Christ. They hold pretty much the same belief in that regard as Catholics.

Baptism is not symbolic. It is a necessary first step toward being saved. According to their theology, then, infant Baptism would be an *essential* doctrine because if we're born again through Baptism, and being born again is necessary for salvation, then for an infant, as for anyone, it would be necessary to be baptized in order for them to get into Heaven. If they died before they were baptized, there could be a problem since being re-generated, or born again, into the Spirit is necessary for salvation. This, again, makes infant Baptism, and Baptism in general, an essential doctrine.

Okay, let's recap: We have some, you could say most, Protestants who believe infant Baptism is merely symbolic, and it is therefore clas-sified by those Protestants as a nonessential doctrine. On the other hand, there are other Protestants who believe Baptism is a necessary step for salvation, and therefore infant Baptism would fall into the category of an essential doctrine.

So who, within all of Protestantism, gets to decide what is an es-sential doctrine and what is a nonessential doctrine? What authority within Protestantism can make that call? Well, since Protestants go by the Bible—and the Bible alone (*Sola Scriptura*)—as their ultimate authority, it seems reasonable to me to believe that there must be some sort of list, table, chart, or something in the Bible itself that identifies and separates the essential doctrines from the nonessential doctrines.

But guess what? There is nothing, absolutely nothing, in the Bible that identifies any doctrine as being essential or as being nonessential. There is nothing in any of the pages of the Bible that speaks to essen-tial versus nonessential doctrines. Saint Paul never added any kind of index to any of his letters that identifies essential versus nonessential doctrines. In fact, since all Protestant doctrines are from the Bible, or so they claim, this whole "nonessential" doctrine thing has to make one ask: "Which part of the Bible, which part of the Word of God, do you consider to be 'nonessential'?" Does not the Word of God say that man shall live "by every word that proceeds from the mouth of God" (Matt. 4:4)? That sort of flies in the face of this whole essential versus nonessential garbage. I have yet to read anywhere in the Bible where it says that "man shall live by every *essential* word that proceeds from the mouth of God, but you can basically ignore all the nonessential words that proceed from the mouth of God."

The problem with all of this, as is usually the problem within Protestantism, is who gets to authoritatively decide who is right and who is wrong when it comes to essential and nonessential doctrines. Or if there is even such a thing as a nonessential doctrine? What authority is there in Protestantism that can settle these disputes? As you've already read elsewhere and will read again in questions yet to come in this book, no such authority exists in Protestantism. Where there is disagreement within Protestantism, one is left with nothing more than this person's fallible interpretation of Scripture versus that person's fallible interpretation of Scripture to try and decide where the truth lies. It turns out that the Bible is not the highest authority in Protestantism. This person's or that person's personal opinions of what Scripture does or does not say are the highest authority within Protestantism.

This whole mess of essential versus nonessential doctrines is, in my opinion, nothing more than an attempt, after the fact, to justify all the divisions within Protestantism. It's sort of a "Hey, this is how we can all get along and ignore all of these monumental differences in our theology and just focus on converting all of those poor, ignorant Catholics" kind of thing. "It's okay if we disagree with those other guys on what is or is not true Christian doctrine and practice, as long as we all agree on the essentials." Didn't Jesus say something about knowing the truth, and the truth will set you free (John 8:32)?

To close: Yes, Protestants can accurately answer the question by saying there is no list, table, or index in the Bible that authoritatively delineates between essential and nonessential doctrines. But should they do so, they are implicitly admitting that there is a huge gaping hole in their theology because (a) the whole essential versus nonessential doctrinal paradigm is thereby admitted as not being biblical—it's been made up by men—and (b) there is no authority within Protestantism that can decide, once and for all, and bind all Protestants with their decision as to what is or is not an essential doctrine.

Who Is Jesus Talking about in Matthew 19:12 When He Says There Are Some Who Will Make Themselves Eunuchs for the Sake of the Kingdom of Heaven?

In Matthew 19:11–12, it says the following: "But he said to them, 'Not all men can receive this precept, but only to those whom it is given. For there are eunuchs who have been so from birth, and there are eunuchs who have been made eunuchs by men, and there are eunuchs who have made themselves eunuchs for the sake of the kingdom of heaven. He who is able to receive this, let him receive it.'"

Well, who is this that Jesus is talking about, these men who have made themselves eunuchs for the sake of the Kingdom of Heaven? First, we need to realize that He's not talking about people who have physically made themselves eunuchs for the sake of the Kingdom. We know this because there is absolutely no circumstance that we can find in Scripture where one would need to physically make oneself a eunuch for the sake of the Kingdom of Heaven.

Rather, Jesus is referring to those who have *spiritually* made themselves eunuchs by taking a vow of celibacy. In other words, men who have given up their right to marital relations with a woman. That's how they have made themselves eunuchs for the sake of the Kingdom of Heaven.

What Jesus said in Matthew 19 fits right in with what Paul says in 1 Corinthians 7:32–34, "The unmarried man is anxious about the affairs of the Lord, how to please the Lord; but the married man is anxious about worldly affairs, how to please his wife, and his interests are divided." Then, in verse 35, Paul says, "I say this for your own benefit, not to lay any restraint upon you, but to promote good order and to secure your undivided devotion to the Lord."

The unmarried man, the "eunuch," is able to devote himself with "undivided devotion" to the Lord and, I would add, to the people of God—all for "the sake of the Kingdom of Heaven." So, the question is: Who is it, as we look around our world today, that fits this profile of men who have made themselves eunuchs for the sake of the Kingdom of Heaven? I'm not trying to pick on anyone here, but let's look at just a few examples of various groups of Christian men. Let's start with Baptist ministers. Have Baptist ministers, in general, made themselves eunuchs for the sake of the Kingdom of Heaven? The answer is, quite clearly, no. What about evangelical ministers? Methodist ministers? Nondenominational ministers? Church of Christ preachers? Have any of these groups of men, as a standard, made themselves eunuchs for the sake of the Kingdom of Heaven? Not that I'm aware of.

In fact, I don't personally know of a single minister or preacher in any Protestant denomination who has made himself a eunuch for the sake of the Kingdom of Heaven. I'm not saying there absolutely aren't any, but they are the exception rather than the rule, and the ones that are out there will be found mostly in the Lutheran and Anglican faith traditions—the two faith traditions that retained more of the beliefs and practices of the Catholic Church than any other Protestant faith tradition.

Who, then, could Jesus be talking about here in Matthew 19? Well, in the Catholic Church, particularly in the Latin Rite, the general rule is that our priests take a vow of celibacy. They have, in essence, made themselves eunuchs for the sake of the Kingdom of Heaven. Very, very interesting. The priests of the Catholic Church, in general (there are exceptions), fulfill Jesus' words here in Matthew 19:12.

So, again, the question is: Who is Jesus talking about when He says there are men who have made themselves eunuchs for the sake of the Kingdom of Heaven?

Oh, and one other thing to note regarding this question: In the passage from 1 Corinthians 7 that I cited regarding the unmarried man being able to give his undivided devotion to the Lord, it also talks about how the unmarried woman is anxious about the affairs of the Lord and able to give her undivided devotion to the Lord as well, how she is concerned with how to be holy in body and spirit, whereas the married woman is anxious about worldly affairs and how to please her husband (v. 34). The married woman, like the married man, has divided interests.

This would lead me to ask as a corollary to the main question above: Do we know of any group, or groups, of women who have given up their right to be married—who have taken vows of celibacy—in order to devote their attention wholeheartedly to the Lord and to being holy in body and spirit as Paul talks about in 1 Corinthians 7? Do we find such women in the Baptist denominations? Any Evangelical denomination? Methodist? Presbyterian? Church of Christ? *Any* Protestant denomination? I have actually heard of some orders of celibate women in the Lutheran and Anglican faith traditions, and there may be others here and there, but it is in the Catholic Church where such women are overwhelmingly found. Also, it is from the Catholic tradition of having orders of women religious from which the practice of the Lutherans, Anglicans, and anyone else is derived.

So, let's say this is a question a few Protestants could answer, but definitely not most of them.

Can a Person Judge Himself as Having Been Saved and, Particularly, as Having Been Saved with Absolute Assurance?

There are a number of Protestant denominations whose doctrine states that any given individual believer can judge himself as being saved and that this salvation he has judged himself as receiving can never be taken away from him; it cannot be lost, no matter what. This doctrine is commonly referred to as the doctrine of Eternal Security, or Once Saved, Always Saved. We've already touched on this doctrine in a previous question, but we'll take a look at it from a different angle here.

This question is based on 1 Corinthians 4:3–5: "But with me it is a very small thing that I should be judged by you or by any human court. I do not even judge myself. I am not aware of anything against myself, but I am not thereby acquitted. It is the Lord who judges me. Therefore do not pronounce judgment before the time, before the Lord comes, who will bring to light the things now hidden in darkness and will disclose the purposes of the heart."

On a number of occasions, I've had people ask me: "If you were to die today, do you have absolute assurance that you would be with God in Heaven?" This is one of those Protestant salvation quizzes, along the lines of: "Have you been saved? Have you been born again?" I respond to them by saying that I am not my own judge, and therefore, it is not my place to pass judgment on myself. To which they say, "Well, that just means you don't have absolute assurance of your salvation, which means you're not saved, which means you're not a Christian, which means you're going to Hell," or something to that effect.

But Paul, right here in 1 Corinthians, says, "I do not even judge myself." If Paul doesn't judge himself, then who are we to judge ourselves as being saved, and not just being saved, but as having absolute assurance of salvation? Again, Paul's words tell us that he doesn't even judge himself, even though, as he says, he is not aware of anything against himself. So, even though he seemed to be pretty sure that he was in good standing with God—he wasn't aware of anything against himself—still he realizes that he is not thereby acquitted, or saved, since it is the Lord Who judges him. It is the Lord Who judges everyone!

Paul goes on to warn his readers to not pronounce judgment before "the time," before the Lord comes. Because when the Lord comes, He is going to bring to light things now hidden in darkness, and He will disclose the purposes of each man's heart.

You know, we human beings are finite beings. However, there is one trait we all seem to have that sometimes comes close to approaching the infinite. We have an almost infinite capacity to fool ourselves. Proverbs 21:2 says the way of a man is right in his own eyes. We human beings have this tendency to find excuses for our sinful behaviors. We are very good at justifying our sinful actions to make them seem, at least to ourselves, that they aren't really sins. So, our ways seem to be right in our own eyes, even if they are not right in the eyes of God.

This is why Paul said not to judge before Jesus returns because God alone knows the human heart through and through, and He will disclose the things now hidden in darkness and the purposes of each man's heart. So, given that we have this tendency to justify our bad behaviors, and given the fact that we don't necessarily know our own heart as well as we think we do, and given that Paul tells us that he didn't even judge himself, that he left judgment to the Lord, then it seems a pretty dangerous thing to go around judging ourselves as being saved and judging others as not. I mean, we could *think* we've been saved when we really aren't saved. We could *think* we've accepted

Jesus Christ into our hearts as our personal Lord and Savior when we really haven't. We could *believe* we have a "saving faith" when we really don't.

So, if we go about judging ourselves as being saved, and then we think we have absolute assurance of salvation, we could actually be setting ourselves up for a really big disappointment. Instead of working out our salvation "with fear and trembling" (Phil. 2:12), as the Bible tells us to do, we could allow ourselves to become spiritual couch potatoes because we have the mistaken notion that we are irrevocably saved when we actually might not be. Once again, Paul didn't even have the arrogance to judge himself. He left that for the Lord, to "he who searches mind and heart" (Rev. 2:23). We should do the same.

This makes the correct answer to this question a resounding: "No! We cannot judge ourselves to be saved with absolute assurance." This is why this is a question Protestants can't answer, because the theology of the vast majority of Protestantism contradicts what Paul says in 1 Corinthians 4:3–5.

Question 12

Do We Have to Do the Will of God to Enter the Kingdom of Heaven?

Matthew 7:21 says, "Not everyone who says to me, 'Lord, Lord,' shall enter the kingdom of heaven, but he who does the will of my Father who is in heaven." This means that the very obvious answer to the question above is: "Yes, we have to do the will of God to enter the Kingdom of Heaven." Jesus is pretty clear on that point in Matthew 7:21. So, why is this a question that Protestants can't answer? *Sola Fide*.

The dogma of *Sola Fide* teaches that, no, we don't have to *do* anything at all in order to enter the Kingdom of Heaven. But Jesus says we have to *do* the will of God in order to enter the Kingdom, in order to be saved. It seems *Sola Fide* conflicts with the Bible here. "Well," someone might say, "doing the will of God just means having faith, accepting Jesus into your heart as your Lord and Savior." Three thoughts on that: (1) Where does the Bible say that doing the will of God is limited to just having faith? Answer: it doesn't. (2) *Doing* the will of God, however you define it, is still an action or series of actions that we do. God doesn't make us do His will, nor does He do it for us. We do it by His grace, but we have to cooperate with that grace. (3) Ephesians 2:8–10, as well as other Bible passages that I'll get into with questions yet to come, tells us that doing the will of God involves more than just making an act of faith.

"For by grace you have been saved through faith; and this is not your own doing, it is the gift of God — not because of works, lest any man should boast" (Eph. 2:8–9). This is usually the first passage of the Bible that Protestants will turn to in order to "prove" that we are saved by faith alone (*Sola Fide*). "See," they say, "we are saved by grace through *faith* and *not* because of works!" Indeed we are.

Unfortunately, the vast majority of Protestants distort the meaning of Ephesians 2:8–9 because they are trying to fit the Bible to their beliefs instead of fitting their beliefs to the Bible. This is why they generally ignore Ephesians 2:10, "For we are his workmanship, created in Christ Jesus for good works, which God prepared beforehand, that we should walk in them." Let's look at Ephesians 2:8–10 a little more closely, and we'll see that it presents absolutely no problem to the Catholic, but it is actually a fairly problematic passage for the Protestant.

Yes, we are saved by grace, through faith, and not by works. Catholic teaching, particularly as found in the Council of Trent, says that we are saved by God's grace alone. We receive the grace of God's free gift of salvation through Baptism, just as the Bible teaches. We receive Baptism either because of our personal faith or, if baptized as babies, through the faith of our parents. Before we receive God's grace through Baptism, nothing—neither faith nor works—merits for us the grace of salvation. That is Catholic teaching. That is biblical teaching. We are saved by grace through faith and not by works. "Amen!" says the Catholic.

However, once we have been saved by the free gift of God's grace received through faith by Baptism, we have to respond to what God has freely given us. We have to open that gift. We have to apply that gift to our lives. We have to cooperate with God's saving grace in our lives. In other words, we have to do God's will for our lives, just as Matthew 7:21 tells us. And God's will for our lives is not just that we have faith but that we also, as Ephesians 2:10 tells us, do the good works that God has prepared for us beforehand, before we were even born!

Okay, let's do a little recap here: Jesus says that we have to do the will of God in order to be saved, in order to enter the Kingdom of Heaven. Ephesians 2:10 tells us that God has prepared some works for us, even before we were born, and He says that we *should* walk in them. Not that we could think about walking in them. Or that it would be nice if we walk in them. No! That we *should* walk in them. Which means it is God's will for us to do these works. (By the way, these works will be different for everyone based on the talents and abilities God has given each person, the life situations they find themselves in, and so forth.)

Now, back to the question. The answer is: "Yes, we have to do God's will to enter the Kingdom of Heaven." Scripture tells us, though, that doing God's will involves walking in these works that He has prepared for us. So, ask your favorite *Sola Fide* Protestant this question: "If we don't do the works that God has willed for us to do, can we be saved? Can we enter the Kingdom of Heaven?" The answer is unequivocally: "No!" If we don't do the works He has prepared for us, that means we are not doing His will. And if we don't do the will of God, Jesus tells us we don't get to enter the Kingdom of Heaven.

Therefore, the problem for the Protestant in answering this question is that to say, "Yes, one has to do the will of God, which includes some set of works God has prepared for us, in order to be saved," contradicts the Protestant dogma of *Sola Fide*, which tells us works have nothing whatsoever to do with our salvation. But if the Protestant says, "No, one does not have to do the will of God in order to be saved," then he clearly contradicts what Jesus says in Matthew 7:21. So, to answer the question as Scripture answers the question results in a contradiction with Protestant theology, but to answer the question in a manner consistent with Protestant theology clearly contradicts Scripture.

Thus, we have a question Protestants can't answer.

Question 13

Do I Have to Provide for My Family
in Order to Be Saved?

This question, as well as the next two questions, are short follow-ups
to Question #12 and really drive home the point that doing the will
of God, which is what we must do in order to be saved (Matt. 7:21),
involves more than just making an act of faith. These few questions,
both individually and especially when taken together, drive a stake
through the heart of the dogma of *Sola Fide*.

As has already been noted, and will be noted a few more times
before we're through, *Sola Fide* teaches that works play no role in our
salvation. We are saved by faith, and faith alone. This means, according
to *Sola Fide* theology, that the answer to the question above is: "No,
you do not have to provide for your family in order to be saved since
providing for your family is quite obviously a work and works play no
role in our salvation. It's a good thing to provide for your family, but
whether you do so or not has no bearing on your salvation."

Yet 1 Timothy 5:8 says this: "If anyone does not provide for his
relatives, and especially for his own family, he has disowned the faith
and is worse than an unbeliever." What happens to unbelievers? According to the theology of most Protestants, unbelievers go to Hell.
So, if you're worse than an unbeliever, that must mean you are in a
pretty low rung of Hell. It's very important to note here: Paul is referring to believers as being worse than unbelievers. You wouldn't say
an unbeliever is worse than an unbeliever. That wouldn't make any

sense. No, it's believers who don't provide for their families that are worse than unbelievers. Believers who are supposedly saved, simply by the fact that they are believers, are said to be worse than unbelievers by not doing what they should do regarding their families.

Plus, Paul says that those he is referring to—those who do not provide for their families—have "disowned" the Faith. You can't "disown" something unless you first "own" it. This means that *Sola Fide* cannot possibly be true. Apparently, part of the works that God has prepared for us beforehand (Eph. 2:10) includes providing for our families (if we are in a position to do so). If we don't provide for our families, we are worse than unbelievers. We will go to Hell even though we have faith. Faith alone does not save the believer who refuses to provide for his family.

That's why this is a question Protestants can't answer, because, once again, the biblical answer to the question contradicts the answer that Protestant *Sola Fide* theology gives to the question.

Question 14

Do We Have to Labor for Anything
That Leads to Eternal Life?

The answer to this question, if *Sola Fide* is indeed true, is: "No, we do not have to labor for anything in order to achieve eternal life, because we are saved by faith alone." The problem, though, is that Jesus, in John 6:27, explicitly tells us to "labor" for the food that endures to eternal life: "Do not labor for the food which perishes, but for the food which endures to eternal life." He further tells us in verse 27 that He Himself will give us this food that endures to eternal life.

At first glance, one might think this is a contradiction. Jesus is going to give us this food, yet He says we are to labor for it. Well, which is it? Is He going to give it to us, or do we have to labor for it? In Protestant theology, this is essentially an either/or kind of situation. Is this food that endures to eternal life a free gift of Christ to us, or is it something we have to work for, something we have to labor for? It needs to be one or the other. It can't be both.

In Catholic theology, however, this is a both/and kind of situation. As stated in Question #12, Catholics believe salvation is a free gift from God; however, once we have received this free gift from God, we have to respond to God's grace with faith and works in order to keep from losing that which was freely given to us. So, yes, Jesus gives us the food that endures unto eternal life, *and* we have to labor for it. Both/and. Catholic theology results in no contradiction here.

Plus, when you realize that verse 27, with its talk of food that endures to eternal life, is part of the passage leading directly to the discussion in John 6:51–58 where Jesus is telling us that the bread (the food) He will give us to eat is His Flesh that He will give for the life of the world (verse 51), and that if we eat His Flesh we will have eternal life (verse 54), then we see how this entire discussion on the bread of life in John 6 fits very nicely with Catholic theology (particularly on salvation and on the Eucharist), as opposed to Protestant theology, which ends up twisting Scripture to try and make it fit with Protestant sensibilities.

The answer to the question above is, according to Jesus: "Yes." According to Protestant theology: "No." That's why this is a question Protestants can't answer.

Question 15

Do You Have to Forgive the Sins of Others in Order to Be Saved?

Ask any Protestant you know if he believes that a person's sins have to be forgiven in order for that person to be saved. The answer, 100 percent of the time, will be: "Yes, a person's sins have to be forgiven, or that person will not be saved." Then ask that same Protestant Question #15 above: Do you have to forgive the sins of others in order to be saved? The answer will come back: "No, since forgiving the sins of others is a work and works play no role in our salvation (*Sola Fide* theology); therefore, you do not have to forgive the sins of others in order to be saved."

That's when you go to Matthew 6 and read to them, out loud, verses 14 and 15: "For if you forgive men their trespasses, your heavenly Father also will forgive you; but if you do not forgive men their trespasses, neither will your Father forgive your trespasses." This is pretty straightforward stuff here. Jesus says that if we do not forgive the sins of those who have sinned against us, then our heavenly Father will not forgive our sins. And as your Protestant friend has already stated, if our sins are not forgiven, then we do not get saved. This means in order to be saved, we have to forgive others of their sins, or our sins will not be forgiven and we will not be saved.

We have a very clear example of this in Scripture. In Matthew 18:23–35, we find the story of two servants. The first servant owes the king some huge amount of money that he cannot pay. The servant begs the king not to punish him and to have patience with him. The king forgives the man's debts. The first servant is "saved." The second servant owes the first servant a much smaller amount than the first servant owed the king. He begs the first servant not to punish him and to have patience with him. The first servant refuses to forgive the man's debt and has him punished. The king finds out about it and is enraged.

Here is what the king says to the first servant: "You wicked servant! I forgave you all that debt because you besought me; and should not you have had mercy on your fellow servant, as I had mercy on you?" (vv. 32–33). The king then reinstated the first servant's debt and had him thrown in prison. Jesus tells us, "So also my heavenly Father will do to every one of you, if you do not forgive your brother from your heart" (v. 35).

Scripture is very clear. If you do not forgive the sins of others, you will not be saved, because God will not forgive your sins. But forgiving the sins of others is a work, or series of works, which means it should have no impact on your salvation one way or the other, according to Protestant theology. This is why this is a question Protestants can't answer.

Most of the time I ask this question, I don't really get much of an answer. The one time someone tried to make a direct response, as opposed to deflecting the question and trying to change the subject, it was essentially that forgiving others' sins was a "consequence" of being saved, not a "cause" of being saved. When I responded that it was very clear from Matthew 6:14–15 that you needed to first forgive the other person's sins before the Father would forgive your sins, the comeback was, "Well, it happens at the same time." I asked, "What happens at the same time?" "Your sins are forgiven by God, and at the same moment, you forgive the sins of others." This "consequence" of salvation was automatic because of course everyone who is saved will absolutely forgive others. So, it's a consequence of your salvation, but it's a consequence that happens at the same time as your salvation. Yeah, right.

That's when I brought Matthew 18 and the story of the two servants into the discussion. "Look," I said, "the king forgives the servant's debts first, and then the servant is saved (debt free). But even after he is saved, he refuses to forgive the debts of the other servant. So, forgiveness of others isn't automatic even after you've been saved, and if you don't forgive others, you can lose that salvation that has already been given to you. It's right there in the Bible!"

What response did I get? "You Catholics just don't know how to interpret the Bible."

This is another question Protestants can't answer.

Question 16

Is There Anything We Can Do to Cover Our Sins?

The immediate answer to this question from most Protestants is an emphatic, "No! There is nothing anyone can do to cover his sins. Jesus' death on the Cross, and that alone, paid the price for our sins." Yet we find in both James 5:20 and 1 Peter 4:8 that there are at least a couple of ways that we can indeed "cover a multitude of sins."

"Let him know that whoever brings back a sinner from the error of his way will save his soul from death and will cover a multitude of sins" (James 5:20).

"Above all hold unfailing your love for one another, since love covers a multitude of sins" (1 Pet. 4:8).

The Word of God tells us that by bringing a sinner back from the error of his ways, we can cover (receive forgiveness from God for) a multitude of *our* sins. The Word also says that by showing love for others, we can cover (receive forgiveness from God for) a multitude of our sins.

Wait a minute, though. Aren't Protestants correct when they say it is Jesus' death on the Cross that alone paid the price for our sins? Yes, they are correct when they say that. However, in the *Sola Fide* theological systems of most Protestants, it is only by believing in Jesus as our personal Lord and Savior (*Sola Fide*) that we can have our sins forgiven. There is no action we can take—nothing we can do—that will result in the forgiveness of our sins. Believing, and believing alone, is all that is necessary.

James 5:20 and 1 Peter 4:8, however, show that kind of thinking to be absolutely contrary to the Word of God. Yes, it is Jesus' death on the Cross that paid the price for our sins. However, if faith alone is what saves us and causes our sins to be forgiven, then those two Scripture verses are rendered void and meaningless. They make no sense if sins are forgiven through faith alone. These two verses show that love plays an important role in the forgiveness of sins. That is stated directly in 1 Peter 4:8, and James 5:20 does so indirectly. For what is the act of bringing a sinner back from the error of his ways if not an act of love?

So, it is not simply through faith alone by which we can cover our sins. It is also by works of love that the Scripture says we can cover our sins. Or as Galatians 5:6 puts it: "For in Christ Jesus neither circumcision nor uncircumcision is of any avail, but faith working through love." Faith *working* through love is of "avail." Faith working through love is found in, for example, Matthew 25:31–46, where the "sheep" feed the hungry, clothe the naked, and visit the sick and the imprisoned, and it results in them being called into the Kingdom. Faith working through love results in the faithful being forgiven by God because they have forgiven others (Matt. 6:14–15). Faith working through love causes the branches of the vine to produce good fruit and not be cut off from the vine (John 15:1–6).

So, yes, according to the Word of God, there are things that we can do—bring a sinner back from the error of his ways and hold unfailing our love for others—by which we can cover a multitude of sins. This flies in the face of Protestant theology, though, which is why this is a question Protestants can't answer.

Question 17

Where Did the Bible Come From?

I've asked this question of Protestants on numerous occasions and received several different answers. "It came from God." "It didn't come from the Catholic Church!" "It came from the early Christians." "I don't know; what does it matter?"

This, folks, is a core question for all Christians, and particularly so for those Christians who believe in the dogma of *Sola Scriptura*—the Bible as the sole rule of faith, or some would say the sole *infallible* rule of faith, for Christians. If we don't know how the Bible came to be, then how can we know it is inspired by God? How can we know that it is inerrant—that is, without error?

Yes, the Bible came from God. But unless God spoke to you directly about it, someone here on earth had to have told you it was from God. Someone here on earth had to vouch for the divine authorship of the Bible. Who was that? What human authority do you rely upon in order to believe that this book we call the Bible is actually the inspired, inerrant Word of God? Who gave us the Bible as we have it today? Whose authority do we rely upon for our belief in the inspiration and inerrancy of the Bible? Whose authority?!

This is a question that most Christians, particularly Protestants, but Catholics as well, seem to have never thought about. Sometimes it seems that folks think it just fell out of the sky one day. God just leaned over a cloud, dropped the Bible out of the sky, and said, "Here it is, people; do your best with it!"

How could such an important question be completely off the radar of so many people who call themselves Christians, and particularly, of so many Christians who claim to go by the Bible alone for their beliefs? I'll tell you how. Because the answer to this question does not reflect all that favorably upon Protestantism. The answer to the question is: the Catholic Church. The Catholic Church gave us the Bible as we have it today. It is the authority of the Catholic Church upon which we rely to believe that the Bible is the inspired, inerrant Word of God.

And that fact doesn't sit too well with Protestants. Here are the facts: Jesus started a church. And He sent the Holy Spirit to guide that church. Which is why we can trust the word of that church. It was founded by Jesus and is guided by the Holy Spirit. It is from that church we received these writings we call the Bible. The question is: What is the name of that church? Well, there is only one church that can historically show it was in existence in the early centuries of Christianity. It wasn't the Baptist Church. Nor was it the Evangelical Church. Nor the Lutheran, nor Anglican, nor Methodist, nor Presbyterian, nor Pentecostal, nor any nondenominational church, nor any other Protestant church. It wasn't the Greek Orthodox Church, the Russian Orthodox Church, or any other of the Orthodox churches.

It was the Catholic Church. The Catholic Church decided which books should and should not be in the Bible. Some of the books we now have in the Bible, both the New Testament and the Old Testament, were the subject of dispute as to whether or not they were truly inspired by God. Other books that are not now in the Bible were being put forth by some Christians as indeed being inspired by God. Someone had to make some decisions. The Catholic Church did just that. The Catholic Church, through its councils and through the office of the pope, put the Bible together, as we have it today, more than three hundred years after Christ.

That is simply a historical fact. It is a historical fact that makes many Protestants a little uncomfortable. Some will deny the Catholic Church had anything to do with the Bible. Yet when I ask them, "Okay, if it wasn't the Catholic Church, then who did put the Bible together?" Response: "The early Christians." "Which early Christians? Can you give some names? What year did they live in? Where were they from? What authority did they have that we should trust their decisions? Were they infallible in their decision-making?" Generally, I receive no response to those questions.

Others will candidly admit, "Yes, yes, it was the Catholic Church that put the Bible together." Then they say, "But not long after that, the Catholic Church went astray and started teaching heresy." Oh, so the Church that was founded by Jesus Christ, guided by the Holy Spirit, and whose authority we rely on to know the Bible is the inspired, inerrant Word of God started teaching heresy not long after it gave the world the Bible. That makes perfect sense. Yeah, right!

One other objection from Protestants regarding the Catholic Church and the Bible goes something like this: "Yes, the Catholic Church gave us the New Testament books of the Bible, but all Christians agree on those books. And it was the Jewish people who gave us the Old Testament books of the Bible, and the Jews don't have those seven books of the Old Testament in their Scriptures that Catholics have in theirs. So, Protestants agree with the Jews on this one."

Well, here's the thing: Since when did the Jewish leaders have the authority to decide matters of religion for Christians? Since when did the Jewish leaders have the authority to decide which books should and should not be included in the Christian Bible? Fifty days after the Resurrection, on the Day of Pentecost, the religious leaders of Judaism lost their authority regarding all matters pertaining to religion over all those who were baptized into the Church. That authority belonged to Peter and the leaders of the Church. From the Day of Pentecost on, the leaders of the Christian religion made decisions for Christians in all religious matters. Jewish authorities had no say in matters pertaining to Christianity.

Those who argue they go by what Judaism teaches about the canon of the Old Testament rather than by what the Catholic Church teaches are being a bit disingenuous. Consider, for example, what would happen if Judaism all of a sudden decided to add another book to their

Scriptures (the Old Testament). Would Protestant leaders say, "Well, if the Jews are adding another book to their Scriptures, then we will certainly add another one to ours, since we go by their decision in all matters pertaining to the Old Testament canon"? Of course, they wouldn't!

Do Protestant churches adhere to the Jewish understanding of the Old Testament? The Jews don't see the Old Testament as pointing to Jesus Christ. The Jews don't see any hint of the Trinity in the Old Testament. Do Protestants agree with them on these matters? Of course, they don't. In other words, Judaism has no authority to determine anything regarding the Old Testament for Christians.

One last comment on this: For Protestants to say that the Catholic Church got it right when deciding on the New Testament but got it wrong when deciding on the Old Testament is pretty fuzzy logic. If the Church could get the Old Testament wrong, then there is absolutely no guarantee it got the New Testament right.

Okay, getting back to the question. The historical fact that it is the authority of the Catholic Church upon which all Christians, Catholic or not, rely for their assurance that the Bible is the inspired, inerrant Word of God makes this a question Protestants can't answer.

Where in the Bible Is the List of the Books That Should Be in the Bible?

This question is a corollary of Question #17 and is yet another question that strikes at the heart of *Sola Scriptura*. The answer to this question shows that the dogma of *Sola Scriptura* has a logical inconsistency at its very core. *Sola Scriptura* tells us that the Bible is the sole authority for all matters pertaining to the Christian Faith. I can't tell you how many times I've heard someone say, "If it's in the Bible, I believe it. If it's not in the Bible, I don't."

So, if you were to ask a Protestant about his beliefs on salvation, he will give you passages from the Bible. If you were to ask a Protestant about his beliefs on the Rapture, he will give you passages from the Bible. If you were to ask a Protestant about his beliefs on the divinity of Jesus, he will give you passages from the Bible. If you were to ask a Protestant about his beliefs on the canon of Scripture (the list of books that should be in the Bible) ... uhmm ... well, guess what? He will *not* give you passages from the Bible. Why not? Because he can't! There is no list in the Bible of which books should be *in* the Bible.

This means, in the early centuries of Christianity, when there were disputes among Christians as to which books should or should not be considered the inspired, inerrant Word of God, did they consult the Bible to decide the disputes? No! They couldn't. Because the Bible is what the disputes were about. So, they had to consult some authority *outside* of the Bible in order to know which books should be on the *inside* of the Bible. The logical conclusion of that fact is that the Bible is *not* the sole authority for all matters pertaining to the Christian Faith because you have to have some authority outside of the Bible in order to have the Bible in the first place!

Now, some might say, and some have said to me, "John, you have misunderstood *Sola Scriptura*. It doesn't teach that the Bible is the sole authority in all matters pertaining to the Christian Faith; rather, it is the sole *infallible* authority in matters pertaining to the Christian Faith. There can be other authority in Christianity, it's just not infallible authority unless it is the Scriptures."

My first response to that is from the Westminster Confession of Faith, which is a founding document of the Methodist Church. Regarding Scripture, it states: "The whole counsel of God concerning all things necessary for His own glory, man's salvation, faith and life, is either expressly set down in Scripture, or by good and necessary consequence may be deduced from Scripture: unto which nothing at any time is to be added, whether by new revelations of the Spirit or traditions of men."

Essentially, this famous Protestant confession of faith says that it's Scripture, and only Scripture, that is authoritative regarding matters of the Christian Faith. But for the sake of argument, let's say there is indeed authority outside of Scripture, just not infallible authority. That still doesn't solve the problem for Protestants that is posed by the question of this chapter. If there is no list of books in the Bible that tells you what books should be in the Bible, then where did that list come from? What authority decided which books were or were not to be included in the Bible?

Furthermore, since whatever authority this was that decided on the canon of Scripture was not infallible — remember, the Bible is the only infallible authority according to these folks — then what assurance do we have that they got it right? What assurance do we have that whoever it was that decided on the canon of Scripture, with whatever so-called authority it was that they had, got it right when it came to which books should and should not be included in the Bible?

Answer: We have absolutely no assurance that they got it right. The best Protestants can do, given their own theology when it comes to the Bible, is to say that they have, as the famous Reformed theologian R. C. Sproul stated, "a fallible list of infallible books." The best Protestants can do is to say that they think, or that they're pretty sure, or that they have genuine hope that the Bible contains all the books it should contain — no more, no less.

So, they *might* have the canon of Scripture, right? Sorry, but that's not good enough. Besides, if there is no authority that can proclaim an infallible list of books for the Bible, what authority is there that can proclaim that every, or even any, book of the Bible is infallible? There isn't. So, what R. C. Sproul should have said is that in Protestantism they have a fallible list of books that they *hope* are infallible … maybe.

The answer to the question is that there is no list anywhere in the Bible of which books should be in the Bible. Which is why this is a question Protestants can't answer, because it causes all sorts of difficulties for that most fundamental of Protestant dogmas—*Sola Scriptura*.

Question 19

How Old Is the Church Jesus Started?

A lot of the mess and confusion regarding doctrine and authority that we find in Christianity today—thanks to the hundreds of thousands upon hundreds of thousands of churches and denominations out there—can be solved with just some good, old-fashioned common sense. That's what the question of this chapter is all about: common sense.

How old is the church Jesus started? Two thousand years old. That's common sense. Jesus lived two thousand years ago. He started a church. So, the church He started has to be two thousand years old, right?

But why is this a question Protestants can't answer? Because there isn't a Protestant church in existence that can claim to be more than about five hundred years old. The Lutheran Church—the oldest of all Protestant churches—started, essentially, in 1517. So, there is no Protestant church or denomination, not a single one, that can claim to be the Church Jesus started two thousand years ago in Israel. Rather, they are all offshoots of the Catholic Church, or offshoots of offshoots of the Catholic Church.

Furthermore, we see in Matthew 16:16–19 that Jesus founded one Church. Just one. And nowhere in the Bible do we see anything about various denominations (divisions) within that one Church founded by Jesus that were out there with their own authority structure and/ or their own body of doctrines and dogma.

I mean, think about it. There is this one Church founded by Jesus and guided by the Holy Spirit. It's cruising along for four or five decades after Jesus' Resurrection. And let's say you're in Corinth or Thessalonica or Galatia around AD 80, and you decide you want to split off from that original Church to form your own denomination. What are you saying? You're saying that there is something not quite right about this original Church that the Holy Spirit is guiding. Maybe you think you can do a better job of guiding the Church than the Holy Spirit is doing. Or maybe you've read the Bible for yourself, and you realized that the original Church has gotten something wrong regarding doctrinal teaching. Really?

No! There were no splits, no divisions, no denominations in the New Testament Church. None. Jesus founded one Church. That Church had no denominations. That Church is two thousand years old. That Church could not have been a Protestant church. This is why this is a question Protestants can't answer.

Question 20

If You Are a Branch of the Vine, Which Is Christ, Can You Be Cut Off from the Vine?

Most Protestants believe in the doctrine of Eternal Security, also known as Once Saved, Always Saved. The essence of this doctrine is that once a person has been saved—through faith alone—he cannot ever be "unsaved." The thinking is that since there was nothing he could do to be saved (*Sola Fide*), there is nothing he can do to be unsaved. The necessary ramification of this doctrine is that sin has no consequences regarding one's salvation. Good works didn't get you saved, so bad works (sins) can't get you unsaved.

John 15, however, doesn't seem to quite agree with this doctrine of Once Saved, Always Saved. In verse 1, Jesus says He is the true vine. He tells the apostles, in verse 5, that they are the branches. Even though He is speaking directly to the apostles at the Last Supper, I don't know of any Christian who doesn't understand that Jesus is speaking to all who follow Him, to all of His followers throughout time. Every believer in Christ is a branch of the vine that is Christ. Every believer in Christ is connected to Christ.

Given that, the question I often ask Protestants is this: "Can you be a branch of the vine, which is Christ, if you are an unbeliever?" I have never come across a Protestant who said, "Yes, unbelievers can be a branch of Christ," even though I've asked that question many, many times. Vine = Christ. Branch of the vine = believer in Christ. Given that, the branches of the vine are, by definition, "saved" according to Protestant theology. You're saved by faith alone. They have faith, they believe, they are saved. So, branches of the vine of Christ are those who have been saved; that's how they become branches of the vine.

This, however, is where the problem comes in. In John 15:2, Jesus says, "Every branch of mine that bears no fruit, he [the Father] takes away." And then in verse 6, He goes on to say, "If a man does not abide in me, he is cast forth as a branch and withers; and the branches are gathered, thrown into the fire and burned." If a branch—a believer, a Christian—does not bear fruit (i.e., good works), the Father takes the branch away. Wait, what? The Father takes the branch away. Away from the vine? That's not possible, is it? A believer is saved. Believers have eternal security. They can't be separated from Christ, right?

What happens to these branches that are taken away from Christ? They wither, and then they are thrown into the fire and burned. Huh? I wonder what that's a reference to. Obviously, it's a reference to Hell. One minute the branch, the believer, is connected to the vine, to Christ. Then after producing no fruit, the vine is cut off from the branch, cut off from Christ, and thrown into Hell. Once Saved, Always Saved? Not happening here.

Now, some have said, "Well, those that were thrown into the fire were never really saved in the first place." Sorry, but that doesn't fit with what John 15 actually says. Nowhere does it say, "The branches My Father takes away are those that didn't really believe." Besides, He calls the ones that are taken away and thrown into the fire "branches." They are branches. Which means they did indeed, at one time, belong to the vine. They were believers. They were saved.

If they had never been believers, then they couldn't be referred to as branches. They would have been called wannabe branches, pseudo branches, fake branches, false branches, or something other than branches. But no, they were referred to as just branches. They were saved. After being saved, they didn't produce fruit—maybe they didn't do the good works that God had prepared for them beforehand (Eph. 2:10)—and so they were cut off from the vine, cut off from Christ, and tossed into the fire and burned. No eternal security. No Once Saved, Always Saved. Yes, one more question Protestants can't answer.

Question 21

What Good Deed Must I Do to Have Eternal Life?

This is a question that was asked directly of Jesus in Matthew 19:16. I don't know of a single Protestant, at least not one who believes in salvation by faith alone, who would answer the question as Jesus did. How did Jesus answer it? "If you would enter life, keep the commandments" (v. 17).

Isn't that strange? Jesus should have said, I would think, "Don't you know there is no good deed you can do to have eternal life? All you have to do is believe in Me, and you will be saved. Accept Me into your heart as your personal Lord and Savior, and that's it—you're saved!" Well, that's what He should have said if *Sola Fide* is true. I mean, *Sola Fide* says that good deeds (works) have nothing at all to do with our salvation. So, Jesus had the absolute perfect opportunity right here in Matthew 19 to set the record straight with His answer to this question. He could have let everyone know, for all time, beyond a shadow of a doubt, that it is faith, and faith alone, by which we are saved.

But He didn't do that, did He? I wonder why? Maybe, just maybe, because *Sola Fide* is a false dogma. It isn't true. Maybe works do indeed play a role in our salvation. Maybe works are indeed a necessary response on our part to the free gift of salvation we receive through Jesus Christ in Baptism. Maybe if we do not do the works that God has prepared for us beforehand to do (Eph. 2:10), then we are not doing the will of God, and if we do not do the will of God, we do not enter the Kingdom of Heaven (Matt. 7:21).

So, ask any Protestant you know this question: "What good deed must I do to have eternal life?" and see if he answers you as Jesus answered the young man who asked Him that question. He won't, at least not if he believes in *Sola Fide*. Then take him to Matthew 19:16–17 and ask him why his answer is different than the answer Jesus gave. It's different because to answer as Jesus answered is to contradict his own theology. This is why this is a question Protestants can't answer.

Question 22

Who Is the Devil Seeking to Devour?

"Be sober, be watchful. Your adversary the devil prowls around like a roaring lion, seeking some one to devour" (1 Pet. 5:8). What a strange thing for Peter to say. "The devil is prowling around like a lion seeking to devour folks." The question is: Why? If once I've been saved there is nothing anyone can do—including the devil, or that even *I* can do—to make me lose my salvation (be devoured by the devil), then isn't the devil just wasting his time?

Now, you might say, "But John, even though the devil can't touch those who have already been saved, there are all those unsaved folks out there that he can devour." Sorry, but that doesn't make any sense, because if they're unsaved, if they haven't accepted Jesus into their hearts as their personal Lord and Savior, then they've already been devoured by the devil. He has no need to "prowl around" seeking them. He knows right where they are. They're sitting on the bench of Team Satan.

Someone else might say, "John, John, Peter is simply warning the faithful to be wary of temptations from the devil and not to give in to them and end up committing a sin. This is not at all a salvation issue." Oh, committing a sin is the equivalent of being "devoured" by the devil?

When a lion devours someone or something, the lion consumes it completely. Not much, if anything, is left after the lion is done devouring its prey. The prey belonged to the lion, and it was completely absorbed into the lion.

So if the devil is like a lion, and he devours someone, it would seem his prey now belongs to him, is totally consumed by him, and is completely absorbed into him, would it not? Doesn't that describe the unsaved? Don't they belong to the devil?

So, 1 Peter 5:8 must not be referring to the unsaved because the devil already has them in his grasp. But we know, according to Once Saved, Always Saved theology, that it can't be the saved that the devil is prowling around for and looking to devour.

So, who is the devil prowling around looking for? That's why this is another question Protestants can't answer.

What Is the Only Pure Offering Ever Offered to God?

"For from the rising of the sun to its setting my name is great among the nations, and in every place incense is offered to my name, and a pure offering; for my name is great among the nations, says the LORD of hosts" (Mal. 1:11).

In Malachi, we see a prophecy of a time that will come after the death and Resurrection of Jesus. We know it's a prophecy because it speaks of God's name being "great among the nations," or the Gentiles. Well, when Malachi was written, some four hundred and fifty years or so before Christ, God's name was not great among the Gentiles. At that time, the Gentiles (the nations) were worshipping all sorts of false gods. It was only after Christ's Resurrection that we see the Gentiles being evangelized (see Acts 10; 11) and God's name eventually being made great among the nations.

This prophecy in Malachi 1:11 also speaks of how, "from the rising of the sun to its setting," incense is offered to the name of the Lord and a pure offering among the nations. Let's stop and think about that for a moment. There will come a time, after the death and Resurrection of Jesus, in the various nations around the world, when incense and a pure offering will be offered to the name of the Lord, all day, every day. This is obviously speaking of some sort of worship ritual, one that occurs over and over again throughout each day among the nations.

What could Malachi be talking about here? Do we know of any kind of worship ritual that was started at some point after Jesus came to live among us, which spread to all the nations—and that is maybe still occurring in our day and age—that might fit the description in Malachi 1:11? To answer that, I think we need to focus on the words *pure offering*. What is Malachi talking about here? What pure offering is being offered to the Lord? Well, again, let's stop and think about that for a moment. What is the only truly pure offering that has ever been offered to God? Isn't the answer to that question pretty obvious? Jesus Christ. Jesus offered Himself on the Cross to the Father in reparation for our sins. Jesus Christ—Savior, Redeemer, Son of God, Son of Man, Lord of lords, King of kings, sinless—is the only truly pure offering that has ever been offered to the Lord.

Given that, do we know of any kind of worship ritual where the sacrifice of Jesus Christ is offered? As a pure offering? Along with incense? Throughout the day? Among the nations? Yes, actually, we do. The Mass. In the Catholic Mass, we offer, we "re-present" the offering, that Jesus made of Himself to the Father. How often does the Mass occur? Pretty much every hour from the rising of the sun to its setting. Where does the Mass occur? In all the nations around the world. The Catholic Mass perfectly fits the prophecy of Malachi 1:11.

This is why this is another question Protestants can't answer, because the *answer* to the question—Jesus Christ is the only pure offering ever offered to God—points directly to the Mass. The Mass that is celebrated from the rising of the sun to its setting in Catholic churches every day in all the nations of the world.

Can a Christian Be Severed from Christ or Fall Away from Grace?

The immediate response to this question from Protestants who believe in the doctrine of Eternal Security (Once Saved, Always Saved) is: "No! A Christian can *never* be severed from Christ or fall away from grace." If that's the case, though, then I'm a little confused by what I find in Galatians 5.

First of all, let me point out that the letter of Paul to the Galatians is written exclusively to believers. Galatians 1:2 tells us that the letter is addressed to the "churches" of Galatia. One can be a member of the church, according to Protestant theology, only if one is a believer. Also, in Galatians 5:1, Paul states that "Christ has set us free." "Us" obviously refers to Paul and those to whom Paul is writing. He says that they've been set free by Christ—that is, set free from sin, saved. So, again, the Galatians are believers. They have been saved.

Yet even though the Galatians are believers, and believers can never lose their salvation (Once Saved, Always Saved), Paul says some odd things to them in chapter 5. In verse 1, Paul warns them to "not submit again to a yoke of slavery." He's talking about submitting again to a yoke of sin, to being slaves of sin. In other words, Paul is warning them against losing their freedom in Christ, losing their salvation, and submitting "again" to a yoke of sin that leads to damnation.

But that's not possible, is it? If Once Saved, Always Saved is true, then believers can never lose the freedom that they have gained in

Christ. They can never "again" submit to a yoke of slavery. So, why does Paul give them this warning? Is he just sort of kidding around with them? Apparently not, because in the very next verse, Paul tells the Galatians that if they receive circumcision, "Christ will be of no advantage to you" (5:2). Come again? They're believers, Paul, how could Christ ever be "of no advantage" to them?

A little background here: What was going on with the Galatians is that they were Gentiles. A group of Jewish Christians, known as Judaizers, were going around to Gentile Christians, such as the Galatians, and telling them that in addition to the Christian teachings and practices they accepted, they also needed to accept certain teachings and practices of Judaism, such as circumcision, keeping kosher, celebrating the Jewish feasts and festivals, and so on. Paul is arguing against what the Judaizers are telling the Galatians.

So, Paul tells the Galatians that if they receive circumcision, and by so doing put themselves under the old law, then Christ will be of no advantage to them. Paul says it even more forcefully in verse 4 when he tells them that if they think they can be justified by "the law," then they are "severed from Christ" and have "fallen away from grace." Whoa!

It is very apparent that the Galatians were "saved," according to Protestant theology. Paul says that they have been set free by Christ—that's pretty saved. Yet if they give in to what the Judaizers are telling them, and try to rely on the old law for their salvation, then Christ will be of no use to them, and they will fall away from grace. Can a saved person ever be said to be someone who has fallen away from grace, or that Christ is of no advantage to them? Of course not. Christ is of every advantage to the saved, and they always have access to God's grace.

The answer to our question, then, is: "Yes, a Christian can indeed be severed from Christ and can indeed fall away from grace, at least according to the Word of God." That's why this is a question Protestants can't answer, because in Once Saved, Always Saved (Eternal Security) theology, the answer is: "No, a Christian can never be severed from Christ or fall away from grace." The Protestant has to contradict his own theology in order to give a scripturally correct answer to this question.

Do We Have to Eat the Flesh of Christ and Drink His Blood to Have Eternal Life?

"No," the Protestant should say, "there isn't anything we have to *do* to receive eternal life!" Yet in John 6:53–54, Jesus says, "Unless you eat the flesh of the Son of man and drink his blood, you have no life in you; he who eats my flesh and drinks my blood has eternal life." Jesus tells us that, yes, we do indeed have to eat His flesh and drink His Blood to have eternal life. Whether you take what Jesus is saying here literally or figuratively, He is saying that there is something we have to *do* in order to be saved—a work, an action. Which puts the lie to the dogma of being saved by faith alone.

The response to that, which I've often heard, is that what Jesus means when He says "to eat his flesh and drink his blood" is we need to eat Him up and drink Him up through our reading of Scripture. Jesus was saying in John 6 that we need to read Scripture and devour Him in Scripture. So, when He tells the apostles to eat His Body and drink His Blood at the Last Supper, what He was really telling them to do was to read Scripture? And when He said, "Do this in remembrance of me," He was referring to reading Scripture? He was telling them to read the New Testament Scripture, which didn't yet exist, as a "remembrance" of Him?

"Well, no, that's different. At the Last Supper, He was telling them to remember His sacrifice for them. That's what the bread and wine symbolize—the giving of His Body and Blood on the Cross." Oh, so in John 6, eating His Body and drinking His Blood = reading Scripture. At the Last Supper, eating His Body and drinking His Blood = remembering His sacrifice on the Cross. Sorry, but that just doesn't fly.

However, another response that I've occasionally heard is that in John 6, what is meant by eating His flesh and drinking His Blood is "to believe in Jesus." Eat Him up. Drink Him up. Believe in Him! That still leaves you, though, with the problem of reconciling eating His Body and drinking His Blood in John 6 with the meaning of eating His Body and drinking His Blood in the accounts of the Last Supper. When Jesus said "do *this*" in remembrance of Him, He was actually saying to believe in Him in remembrance of Him? I don't think so. That makes no sense. When He says "do *this*" at the Last Supper, "this" refers to a specific action: the distribution of His Body and Blood (again, whether you take that symbolically or literally). It does not refer to accepting Him into your heart as your personal Lord and Savior.

But for the sake of argument, let's say that when Jesus says in John 6 we must eat His flesh and drink His blood to have eternal life, He really does mean we must believe in Him. It is still an action that Jesus is saying we must take. We must *do*. This would reinforce what Jesus says in John 6:27–29 about how *believing* itself is a work. It's a work of God, but it's a work that we must do. God doesn't do it for us.

In conclusion, no matter how you interpret John 6:53–54—literally, symbolically, to read Scripture, to believe in Jesus, or whatever strange interpretation you may come up with—it is evidence against the dogma of *Sola Fide*. It is evidence that there is something we have to do in order to gain eternal life. This is why this, too, is a question Protestants can't answer.

Question 26

Can an Incomplete Faith Save You?

This is a question that, when I ask it, most people respond with, "What? What do you mean an 'incomplete' faith?" Well, what I mean is this: James 2:22 says, "You see that faith was active along with his [Abraham's] works, and faith was completed by works." The Bible tells us that Abraham's faith was "completed" by works. This would lead me to believe, based on Scripture, that faith without works is incomplete. Thus the question: Can an incomplete faith—faith without works, *faith alone*—save you?

Of course, the initial Protestant thought is to respond with a yes, that faith alone does indeed save you. However, when you describe faith alone as being an "incomplete" faith per James 2:22, there is a little bit of hesitation to respond in the affirmative. So, they have to do some explaining first.

"Wait a minute, John," many Protestants have said, "James 2 is not talking about a 'saving' faith; it's talking about an 'intellectual' faith, a faith that cannot save you." In order to get around the very plain teaching of the Bible, particularly as given in the Letter of James, Protestant theology has had to drive a wedge between the faith James is speaking of in his letter—supposedly a purely "intellectual" faith that does not result in salvation—and the faith that Paul is speaking of in the Letter to the Romans, a "saving" faith that will indeed result in salvation.

There are just a few small problems with that reasoning. First of all, James 2:1 speaks of these people James is writing to as holding "the faith of our Lord Jesus Christ." So, the context of James 2 is the faith of our Lord Jesus Christ. Is not the faith of our Lord Jesus Christ a "saving" faith? Of course, it is! So, this distinction many Protestants try to make between the faith in James and the faith in Romans is nothing more than a rather poor attempt at justifying a belief in *Sola Fide*.

Second, it can further be shown that this attempt to draw a distinction between a "saving" faith in Romans and a merely "intellectual" faith in James is bogus because in chapter 2, James is using the example of the faith of Abraham (vv. 21–23). In a remarkable "coincidence," it just so happens that Paul uses the same example of Abraham's faith in Romans 4:9–22. So, James and Paul are both talking about the faith of Abraham. Was Abraham's faith a "saving" faith in Romans 4 but only an "intellectual" faith in James 2? Of course not! The "saving" faith of Abraham that Paul is talking about in Romans 4 is the same faith of Abraham that James is talking about in James 2, a "saving" faith. To say otherwise would just be ridiculous.

Another point to make is this: Where in James 2 does it use the phrase "intellectual faith"? It doesn't. That phrase is, again, something that is simply made up to try and salvage the dogma of *Sola Fide* in spite of the very clear biblical teaching against it here in the Letter of James (and elsewhere in Scripture). By the way, where do the words *intellectual faith* appear anywhere in the Bible? Guess what? They don't appear in the Bible.

The only kind of faith that is mentioned in the Bible as being a faith that *does not save* is a faith that is not accompanied by works. In other words, a faith that is alone. Faith alone (faith without works) is faith that is not complete and that does not save.

"So faith by itself, if it has no works, is dead" (James 2:17).

"Do you want to be shown, you foolish fellow, that faith apart from works is barren?" (James 2:20).

"For as the body apart from the spirit is dead, so faith apart from works is dead" (James 2:26).

And, again, "You see that faith was active along with his works, and faith was completed by works" (James 2:22).

So read this question to your Protestant friends, family members, coworkers, whoever, and see how they go about trying to twist the Scriptures with this false dichotomy between the faith in James and the faith in Romans in order to make their *Sola Fide* theology work.

This is one more question Protestants can't answer.

Where in the Bible Does It Say We Are Saved, or Justified, by Faith Alone?

I was going to include this in Question #26, but I thought it deserved its own chapter. Think about this. The dogma of *Sola Fide* (salvation by faith alone) is one of the two pillars of Protestantism (*Sola Scriptura* being the other). Not all Protestants believe in this dogma, but the vast majority of them do. This dogma goes back five hundred years to Martin Luther himself. It is foundational to Protestantism.

Given all of that, one would think that we would have no trouble finding verses in Scripture that tell us that we are saved, or justified (the same thing as being saved in Protestant theology), by "faith alone" since Protestants get their theology straight from the Bible, and the Bible alone. So, it might be kind of surprising to some to learn that the phrase "faith alone" appears only *one* time in all of Scripture. What is even more surprising, even shocking, is that the one verse that contains the phrase "faith alone" completely contradicts Protestant theology. Here it is: "You see that a man is justified [saved] by works and not by faith alone" (James 2:24). *Not by* faith alone!

It seems the Holy Spirit inspired James to include in his epistle the exact opposite of one of the foundational dogmas of Protestantism. The only time the phrase "faith alone" appears in the Bible is to tell us that we are *not* saved by faith alone. I find that rather remarkable. It also helps me to understand why Martin Luther was not a big fan of the Letter of James.

What Protestants will argue in response goes back to what I mentioned in Question #26—this whole thing about a "saving" faith versus an "intellectual" faith. But as I pointed out in Question #26, that argument simply does not hold any scriptural water. It's a contrived argument that Protestants had to come up with in a desperate attempt to keep *Sola Fide* from being completely blown apart by James 2 (as well as many other Scripture verses). As I pointed out in Question #1, a dead body is still a body; it's just dead. So dead faith is still faith; it's just dead. So, faith apart from works is dead (James 2:26).

Protestants will also say, though, that there are indeed Bible verses that teach salvation by faith alone, even if the phrase "faith alone" isn't actually used in those verses. Here are a few examples of the "faith alone" verses they will cite:

"For God so loved the world that he gave his only Son, that whoever believes in him should not perish but have eternal life" (John 3:16). "See," they say, "all you have to do to have eternal life is to believe—*Sola Fide.*" They make that argument while they ignore Matthew 19:16–17, where Jesus tells the young man to "keep the commandments" if he wants to have eternal life. So, why isn't it *Sola Praecepta* (Commandments Alone) instead of *Sola Fide*? Because that doesn't fit their preconceived theology.

"For we hold that a man is justified by faith apart from works of law" (Rom. 3:28). Again, they'll say, "See, it's all about faith. Works have nothing to do with one's justification." Ignoring, of course, that "works of the law" is referring to the Old Testament works of the law, such as circumcision, keeping kosher, animal sacrifices, and so on, and does not refer to good works in general. They also ignore, of course, the verse mentioned above, James 2:24, which says we are justified by works and not by faith alone. How about *Sola Labors* (Works Alone)?

"For by grace you have been saved through faith; and this is not your own doing ... not because of works, lest any man should boast" (Eph. 2:8–9). The key phrase they will highlight is: "not because of works." Yet they will ignore verse 10 of Ephesians 2, discussed in Question #12, which says that God has prepared good works for us beforehand, that we should walk in them. They also ignore Romans 2:6–7, discussed in Question #3, which tells us God will render to every man according to his works. To those who "seek for glory and honor and immortality, [God] will give eternal life."

Whatever verse the Protestant throws your way to "prove" we are saved by faith alone, just notice that nowhere is the actual phrase "faith alone," nor can you even find the word "alone." Furthermore, as shown above, any number of verses that speak to the role of works in our salvation have to be completely ignored or interpreted in such a way as to render them nonsensical.

The answer to the question is: There is no verse anywhere in the Bible that states we are saved or justified by faith alone. This is why this is a question Protestants can't answer.

If I Were to Deny That the Letter to the Hebrews Is Inspired Scripture, by What Authority Would You Declare Me Wrong?

The question of authority, as I always say, is the question at the foundation of all doctrinal disputes between Catholics and Protestants. Whether the topic is Mary, the pope, Purgatory, Sacred Tradition, the sacraments, the Rapture, *Sola Scriptura, Sola Fide,* or anything else, it all comes down to the question of who gets to decide.

Is there any authority, in all of Christendom, that can decide a doctrinal (or moral) issue and have that decision be binding on all Christians? Is there any authority, in all of Christendom, that can exercise the power of binding and loosing that Jesus gave to His Church (see Matt. 16:19; 18:18)? If not, then why did Jesus give such authority to the Church if He knew there would not be anyone able to wield that authority? That doesn't make any sense.

Did Jesus establish a Church with the authority to decide doctrinal and moral disputes between its members, or did He leave a toothless Church whose doctrinal and moral teachings are subject to the whims of anyone and everyone who can pick up a Bible and read it for themselves to decide right doctrine and true morality, on their own, without having to answer to any outside authority? Does the Church Jesus founded have binding authority in these matters or not?

Within Protestantism, there is no church or denomination that I have ever come across—and I have come across many—that claims to have the authority to bind on earth that which is bound in Heaven and to loose on earth that which is loosed in Heaven. There is no authority within Protestantism, that I am aware of, that claims to be able to make decisions on matters of doctrine and morality that are then binding on all Christians. Heck, there are Protestant denominations that don't even claim to be able to make decisions on doctrinal or moral teachings that are binding on their own members!

This means that if I were to deny that the Letter to the Hebrews is inspired Scripture, there is no authority within all of Protestantism that could tell me I'm wrong. There would, of course, be plenty of Protestant pastors and theologians, as well as the regular folks sitting in the pews, who would indeed tell me I'm wrong, but not a single one of them would have more authority than what I have. Not a single person or institution within Protestantism would have the authority to bind me to believe that the Letter to the Hebrews is inspired Scripture. *Not one.*

Many would, of course, cite Revelation 22:19 to me, regarding the warning about taking away "from the words of the book" and, therefore, I cannot remove Hebrews from the Bible. But that would not be a sufficient response because (1) I could claim that verse is simply talking about the Book of Revelation; (2) if Hebrews isn't truly inspired Scripture, then it's not truly a part of the Bible, so I wouldn't actually be taking anything away from this book we call the Bible; (3) I could simply claim that the Book of Revelation is also not inspired Scripture.

Not having an authority within Protestantism that can deliver doctrinal and moral decisions that are binding on all Protestants is the reason there exist tens of thousands upon tens of thousands of divisions within Protestantism.

This is another question Protestants can't answer.

Question 29

Do I Have to Love God
in Order to Be Saved?

I addressed this question in one of the chapters in the first part of this book, but I wanted to bring it up again here to emphasize just how easy it is to show the utter bankruptcy of the dogma of *Sola Fide*.

If the Protestant says, "Yes, you have to love God in order to be saved," then he has just admitted that it is not by faith alone that one is saved. It is by faith and love that one is saved. Or as Galatians 5:6 puts it, "In Christ Jesus neither circumcision nor uncircumcision is of any avail, but faith working through love."

But if the Protestant says, "No, you don't have to love God in order to be saved," which is what *Sola Fide*, by definition, teaches, then how ridiculous is that! You can get to Heaven without loving God? You can spend all eternity in Heaven without loving God? Really?

Now, the Protestant response will be, "John, if you don't love God, then that's a sign that you don't really have faith." Oh, where does the Bible say that love of God is a sign of faith but loving God doesn't really have an impact on your salvation? The problem for the Protestant is that the definition of *Sola Fide* is that faith *alone* saves you. Love, by definition, has no impact on your salvation, none. Faith, and faith alone, saves you.

So, the Protestant will answer, "If you have faith, you *will* love God," but he cannot answer that love of God is necessary for salvation, at least not if *Sola Fide* is true.

The *Sola Fide* Protestant answer to this question is: "No." That answer, however, contradicts so much of the Word of God that this, too, is a question Protestants can't answer.

Question 30

How Many Types of Sin Are There?

Protestant theology tells us that all sin is the same. Lying, cheating, stealing, fornication, adultery, worshipping false gods, murder, and so on are all the same before God. I couldn't tell you how many times I have heard the phrase "sin is sin" when discussing this question with Protestants. Just on a common sense level, though, that doesn't make any sense. A ten-year-old walking through the checkout line with his mom at a grocery store steals a pack of gum, and I'm supposed to think that is the same before God as Adolf Hitler killing millions of people in the gas chambers? I don't think so.

But in the world of salvation by faith alone, that's the way it is. As has been discussed elsewhere, Protestant theology teaches, essentially, that sin has no consequences regarding a person's salvation. We're saved by faith alone, and that's that. Sin, other than the sin of unbelief, does not matter when determining one's salvation. This is why a child stealing a pack of gum is the same in God's eyes as the murder of millions of people. "Sin is sin." Again, though, that just doesn't make sense to me.

It is true, however, that God's ways are not our ways. So even though in my mind, as we say here in the South, "That dog don't hunt" from a common sense point of view, or even regarding the concept of justice, I understand that my thoughts and opinions are just that — my thoughts and opinions.

The thing is, though, we can draw on more than just my thoughts and opinions to answer this question. The Bible says, "If anyone sees his brother committing what is not a mortal sin, he will ask, and God will give him life for those whose sin is not mortal. There is sin which is mortal; I do not say that one is to pray for that. All wrongdoing is sin, but there is sin which is not mortal" (1 John 5:16–17). The Bible very clearly tells us that there is sin that is mortal (that kills) and there is sin that is not mortal (that does not kill). Catholic theology calls the sin that does not kill "venial sin."

The King James Bible puts it this way: "There is a sin unto death: I do not say that he shall pray for it. All unrighteousness is sin: and there is a sin not unto death" (1 John 5:16–17 KJV.) No matter the particular translation, it is quite clear that the Bible makes a distinction between two types of sin: (1) mortal sin, which is sin "unto death," and (2) venial sin, which is sin "not unto death." And it's not talking about physical death here; it's talking about spiritual death. In other words, there is sin that will kill the soul, and there is sin that will not kill the soul. This passage from 1 John most definitely does not say, or even so much as imply, "sin is sin." Which is why Protestants can't answer this question.

If there is sin that can kill the soul, sin unto death, then that doesn't bode well for the legitimacy of either *Sola Fide* or Once Saved, Always Saved, does it? If there is sin that can kill the soul, then that means the soul was alive before the sin that can kill it was committed. The soul is alive, saved. Mortal sin is committed and kills the soul. The soul is dead, unsaved. The ramification for Once Saved, Always Saved is obvious: it is a false doctrine. If there exists sin that can lead unto death for the soul, then that means a soul that is saved can indeed become a soul that is un-saved. Boom! Once Saved, Always Saved/Eternal Security is blown apart.

Plus, if there is a sin a person can commit that will cause him to lose his salvation, then *Sola Fide* cannot be true either, because it teaches that there is nothing anyone can do to gain his salvation, and there is nothing anyone can do to lose his salvation. You either have faith, in which case you're saved, or you don't have faith, in which case you are unsaved. Sin is not a determining factor one way or the other.

The Bible says there are two types of sin: sin that is deadly and sin that is not deadly. Protestant theology says otherwise. Which should we believe?

About the Author

John Martignoni is the founder and president of the Bible Christian Society, an apologetics and evangelization apostolate that reaches hundreds of thousands of people each year across the United States and throughout the world with the truths of the Catholic Faith. John is a native of Huntsville, Alabama, who grew up Catholic but never really learned his Faith as a child. He ended up leaving the Catholic Church when he attended the University of Alabama, where he received an undergraduate degree in finance and an M.B.A. He returned to the Faith 13 years later, when he was leaving the University of North Carolina after a year of study in the Ph.D. program in finance.

A few years after coming back to his Faith, John heard an exceedingly anti-Catholic program on a local Evangelical radio station in Birmingham. He called the station to complain, one thing led to another, and a few months later, he was hosting the *Bible Christian Hour*—a weekly, live, call-in program of Catholic apologetics on the largest Evangelical radio station in Alabama. Thus was born the Bible Christian Society and a career in apologetics and evangelization.

Since then, John has spoken at hundreds of parishes and conferences around the country, and a couple of million copies of his talks have been distributed via CD, MP3 downloads, and cassettes (back in the day). For 17 years, he hosted EWTN Radio's *Open Line*, which was heard on hundreds of stations around the country, and he has founded and run Catholic radio stations in Alabama. He has a regular e-newsletter—*Apologetics for the Masses*—that has more than 60,000 subscribers in all 50 states and in more than 80 countries around the world. He is currently the director of evangelization for the Diocese of Birmingham in Alabama.